TRAUMA LITERATURE
Reflections and Ruminations

TRAUMA LITERATURE
Reflections and Ruminations

Editors
N. U. Lekshmi and Rohini K. Potti

AUTHORSPRESS

Worldwide Circulation through Authorspress Global Network
First Published in 2022
by
Authorspress
Q-2A Hauz Khas Enclave, New Delhi-110 016 (India)
Phone: (0) 9818049852
E-mail: authorspressgroup@gmail.com
Website: www.authorspressbooks.com

Trauma Literature: Reflections and Ruminations
ISBN 978-93-5529-137-0

Printed in India at Thomson Press (India) Limited

Dedicated to all
who have traversed through the realms of Trauma

"We are threatened with suffering from three directions: from our body, which is doomed to decay..., from the external world which may rage against us with overwhelming and merciless force, of destruction, and finally from our relations with other men... This last source is perhaps more painful to use than any other." (p77)

– **Sigmund Freud**, *Civilisation and Its Discontents*

Foreword

Trauma is the Greek word for "wound". Although the Greeks used the term only for physical injuries, nowadays *trauma* is just as likely to refer to emotional wounds. We now know that a *traumatic* event can leave psychological symptoms long after any physical injuries have healed. The psychological reaction to emotional trauma now has an established name: *post-traumatic stress disorder,* or PTSD. It usually occurs after an extremely stressful event, such as wartime combat, a natural disaster, or sexual or physical abuse; its symptoms include depression, anxiety, flashbacks, and recurring nightmares.

Trauma is the response to a deeply distressing or disturbing event that overwhelms an individual's ability to cope up feelings of helplessness, diminishes their sense of self and their ability to feel a full range of emotions and experiences. It does not discriminate and it is pervasive throughout the world. The field of trauma studies in literary criticism gained significant attention in 1996 with the publication of Cathy Caruth's *Unclaimed Experience: Trauma, Narrative, and History* and Kali Tal's *Worlds of Hurt: Reading the Literatures of Trauma.* The evolution of trauma theory in literary criticism might best be understood in terms of the changing psychological definitions of trauma as well as the semiotic, rhetorical, and social concerns that are part of the study of trauma in literature and society

There are three main types of trauma: Acute, Chronic, or Complex. Acute trauma results from a single incident. Chronic trauma is repeated and prolonged such as domestic violence or abuse. Complex trauma is exposure to varied and multiple traumatic events, often of an invasive, interpersonal nature. Literary trauma studies is a rapidly developing field which examines how literature deals with the personal and cultural aspects of trauma and engages with such historical and current phenomena as the Holocaust and other genocides, 9/11, climate catastrophe or the still unsettled legacy of colonialism (Rutledge). *Trauma Literature: Reflections and Ruminations* is a jointly edited volume by editors namely Dr. NU Lekshmi and Dr.

Rohini K Potti. It is a volume of scholarly papers on the world's most confronted issues in Literature i.e. Trauma. As we are aware that Trauma Literature is a production of the deeply distressing or disturbing experience, we can well assume the multi-dimensional influences and impacts in lives too. Anything that disturbs us mentally or wounds us physically can be taken to be traumatic. In medical terminology, 'trauma' is said to treat patients of emergency care and attention. We have an emergency ward and route to take the patients. An accident on the road can be painfully traumatic. It is called 'emergency'. If emergency or seriousness becomes the soul of literature, then trauma too impacts our lives in real life. Literature is the vehicle of these experiences in endless pages of narration by writers who have seen, felt and experienced them. But I see victims become the first hand narrators of bitter experiences. For example, the holocaust of Indian partition in 1947 caused a great traumatic experience, first by the victims who themselves became the eye-witnesses and later by the writers who either lived during those times or victims of partition. Such is the impact of Trauma Literature. In fact, all modern literature bear references to trauma episodes. There is no life without trauma. Each one of us has to overcome trauma in the life. These traumatic experiences constitute an important element of literature. Trauma becomes an interdisciplinary study of literature.

The world today is passing through an unprecedented human calamity by a trauma called "Corona pandemic". It has ravaged the lives across the globe. It has become a global calamity. People live in constant fear and psychological grip of pandemic times. An episode of this kind will haunt the minds of people by fear, tensions and emotions as the world has witnessed a series of lockdowns and a couple of health emergencies by first two waves. The times were really challenging and frustrating because of trauma. It has left behind many questions that have mentally occupied the minds. What rules the minds is traumatic effect of pandemic that causes millions of deaths. It becomes a sort of psychological trauma that I experienced as a citizen. Deaths go uncountable each day. Infections by Corona virus become the prime time news across the globe. It makes a good trauma at the beginning of attack. Vaccination drives, though a big relief, warrant compulsory use of masking and sanitisation. All these speak of man in the centre of "trauma".

Coming to this critical volume, I reckon that the Editors have really worked for the collection of research papers. It shows their sincerity and devotion. They cover all aspects of Trauma Literature from different countries. If we look at the overall contributions, we find them highly diverse, innovative and different in settings and themes. They are sizeable in number and rich in content. If variety becomes the spice of life, this collection speaks it all in full vivacity, and splendour. The contributors have covered the race, gender, continents and people who used power to victimize individuals in a few papers. Any civilisation witnessed blood baths in its long history. Trauma Literature is no exception. If man becomes the cause of traumatic events, it is his fellow citizen who is victimized. All types of trauma –physical, psychological, emotional, racial and communal become a perfect focus and nucleus in the collection. Themes and characters typically define the collection, and in particular centre on traumatic developments. I find that there is no deviation from mainstream depictions. Amalgamation and synthesis hold the key to this critical volume which I see a gem of scholarly contributions by the renowned critics and research scholars. Towards the objective of Trauma Literature, the Editors have really been successful in this venture since editing a volume demands patience and commitment. I appreciate them for their scholarly labour in bringing out a successful book at the end.

Dr. P.V. Laxmiprasad
Indian Scholar
Telangana

Contents

Introduction

Trauma in literature addresses the varied forms of human sufferings. Trauma refers to a person's emotional response to an overwhelming event and it also points out how the event consequently affects the individual's sense of self. Trauma theory gained significance in the mid-twentieth century and it gradually occupied a significant role in all important fields of study including Psychoanalysis, Psychology, Humanities and Literature. *Trauma Literature: Reflections and Ruminations* is a collection of articles that document trauma as mirrored in literature.

Dr Sheeba S. Nair in *"Trauma of Prejudice: Gender and Racial Discordance in Sue Monk Kidd's The Secret Life of Bees"* speaks about Trauma Literature, as an offshoot of Diaspora Literature that has begun to address in its course all forms of human suffering. Her paper focusses on Sue Monk Kidd's *The Secret Life of Bees,* a work of fiction that records the trauma of a fourteen-year-old motherless girl Lily and her struggle to exist with her cruel father. The study forges to trace how the Civil Rights Movement implemented to ensure racial equality, aggravated racial intolerance and how people of both the races suffered over it besides addressing the trauma of a teenager in a gender conscious society.

Dr. Manju R. in "Transcending the Collective Trauma of 9/11: Susan L. Roth's *It's Still a Dog's New York: A Book of Healing"* reflects on how Susan L. Roth's *It's Still a Dog's New York: A Book of Healing* provides a blue print for who we should be in such times of crisis, how we should behave, feel and think about what has happened and about our futures. The study authenticates that *It's Still a Dog's New York: A Book of Healing,* functions as a post-9/11 narrative by attempting to heal the traumatised minds of children of New York and instill in them the spirit of optimism and courage to move on with their lives.

As a reflection of reality, Soubhagya S.P. and Dr.N. U. Lekshmi in "Quest of the Traumatised Self: A Revelation of Emigrant Issues" trace the existential struggles encountered by the protagonist Najeeb and other emigrants in order to survive under the cruel treatment of their masters in a land very much alien to them. Dealing with a very relevant issue Asha P. V. in "Rising Like a Phoenix: Narratives on Acid Attack in India" reveals through her paper that acid attack against women is on the rise. The paper analyses the biography *Being Reshma: The Extraordinary Story of an Acid Attack Survivor Who Took the World By Storm* by Reshma Querishi and the 2019 Malayalam movie *Uyare* directed by Manu Ashokan. These narratives are read through the lens of trauma theory. The paper sheds light into the acid attack victims' traumatic experiences and how they deal with it.

"Traversing through the Psyche: Reading of *Never Have I Ever* as a Trauma Narrative" by Anju M. B. explores the representation of trauma in popular culture. She attempts to analyse the subtle undertones of a complex trauma in the comedy drama. The unexpected death of a dear one is traumatic when the deceased person's memories enslave the mind and disrupt the emotions. Athira S.S. in "Traumatising Love: An Exploration of K. R. Meera's *The Poison of Love*" reflects on the representation of traumatic events like Holocaust, World Wars, and 9/11. Her paper on *The Poison of Love* written by K. R. Meera tries to bring into light how Tulsi's innocent love for Madhav becomes the cause for her major traumatic struggles and how it leads to her tragic end.

"Memory, Body and Women: Trauma in Nalini Malani's Art" by V. Kezia Anna reads into the aspects that make a dialogue on the experiences of trauma. Her paper sheds light on the experiences, memories and ideologies across time and space and highlights the pain, suffering, mutilation, dissections and disfigurations. K.S.Chitra's "The Psychological Conflict Underwent by the Mother in *Mother Of 1084*" focuses on the extreme end to which a person could be led, after undergoing so many conflicts in life mentally, physically, socially and emotionally.

Focussing on binary gender classification Monisha M. and B.Sajeetha in "The Concept of Ostracism: Incessant Trauma in the Lives of LGBT" argues that LGBT people are more likely to face intolerance, discrimination, harassment, and violence than heterosexuals as a result of their sexual orientation. The study aims to bring attention to the LGBT community's sufferings, discrimination, prejudice, and marginalisation; to identify the LGBT community's social position and to clarify everyday difficulties. It also highlights the various types of ostracism and their possible consequences for LGBT individuals.

With reference to Africana Womanism, Nayana N. V. in "Cross-Cultural Aspects of Africana Womanism: A Philosophical Overview" explores and analyses Africana Womanism presented by Clenora Hudson-Weems. Africana Womanism is an authentic theoretical concept designed for all women of African descent. Neethu A.Nair's and N. U. Lekshmi's "Encapsulation of Traumatic Experiences: A Reading of Peter Handke's *Repetition*" depicts the unbearable trauma of the narrator through struggles of memories, flashbacks, emotional, domestic violence, and introspection. The paper analyses how Peter Handke, a Nobel Prize winner illustrates many nameless narrators who fall victims to trauma.

Dealing with the life of refugees, Rajasree R. in "The Myth of Returning Home: *Sea Prayer* as a Narrative of Refugee Trauma" reflects on how refugees undergo the trauma of near death experiences and an array of catastrophic events. The paper tries to analyse how the text mediates such traumatic experiences as a narrative of refugee trauma, transmitting it across generations and cultures.

Soumya S.J. In "Female Trauma in Margaret Atwood's *Oryx and Crake*" brings to the lime light that though men and women are equally affected by trauma, women are affected more. The study authenticates through Margaret Atwood's *Oryx and Crake*, that the female characters face many traumatic situations in their lives.

"Trauma Narratives and Herstories in K R Meera" is an in depth study by Dr. Reji A.L. that describes dynamic conditions and possibilities of meaning while interacting with history and memory. The study reveals that fragmented narrative and subject positions unfold painful and humiliating experiences of traumatized individuals. Sajena A. and Sheeba S.Nair in "Abominated and Alienated: The Trauma of the Immigrants in Paolo Bachigalupi's *The Drowned Cities*" through the research paper explore the quandaries faced by the immigrants and their longing to escape to a better place and to lead a peaceful life free from oppression and abhorrence. "Imposed Reticence: A Delve into J. M. Coetzee's *Disgrace" by* Sreelatha. R. H. purely focuses on the plight of the two main female characters. The paper analyses the novel in the framework of Trauma theory and travels through the least touched notion of the traumatised mind that is, silence. The paper also attempts to emphasize the importance of self-expression of an interrupted mind.

Sheethal Tresa Joseph in "Tale of Trauma: The Resurfacing of the Past in Neil Gaiman's *The Ocean at the End of the Lane",* attempts to explore how stories and magic may pervade our real world in a beneficial way and represents how the protagonist's reality as a child and as an adult is shaped by a variety of tangible and invisible objects, through the lens of trauma studies. The effect of retrospective journey plays deeply with the aspects of memory which makes the plot a darkly enchanting tale about memory and childhood.

"Locating the Relocated: A Psychoanalytic Perspective on Jamaica Kincaid's *Lucy"* a paper by M. Vijila Thanga Malar and Dr. R. Janatha Kumari focuses on Kincaid's novel *Lucy* and the various journeys the characters undertake for a better life. Freud's Topographical Model and Structural Model is used for making this analysis evocative. M.M.Shameema and Rohini K.Potti in "*Shuggie Bain*: A Tale of Trauma Portrayed by Douglas Stuart" emphasise the traumatic journey of Shuggie and his family where the psychological problems they faced are discussed carefully.

The collected papers are a true representation of trauma that humanity undergo. Literature as a realistic reflection of life authenticates the traumatic experiences that has been struggling the psyche.

CHAPTER 1

The Life of Strife: The Trauma of Deprived Love Portrayed in Sue Monk Kidd's *The Secret Life of Bees*

Dr. Sheeba S. Nair

Sue Monk Kidd, a distinct voice from the soil of Georgia has won considerable attention from the global readers with her debut novel *The Secret Life of Bees* which was translated into more than twenty-three languages. Being a world hit, it was also made into a film which like the book, enjoys the reputation of a modern classic. The fiction based on the American Civil Rights movement of 1964 tells the story of a motherless child Lily Owens who is fourteen-year-old. Through the travel that the protagonist attempts with her nanny Roseline, a black woman, the novelist strives to present the racial prejudice, suspicion and restlessness that aggravated in the south of America, besides the emotional turmoil and trauma of a teenager.

Trauma literature customarily attempts to excavate the various distressing occurrences or experiences encountered by people in general based on gender and racial inequality, physical illness, holocaust and so on. Michelle Balaev rightly opines that, the term trauma literature refers to a work "that conveys profound loss or intense fear on individual or collective levels" (web). This paper primarily tries to focus on the trauma caused by the loss of a mother in the life of the protagonist Lily Owens who becomes the cause of her death though not intentionally, the physical and psychological torments she undergoes because of this individual loss besides her fear for her father and how she strives through all these troubles.

The Secret Life of Bees portrays Lily as a victim of a patriarchal society where she suffers under a dominating father who cares little about this motherless child. The United States of America, though proclaiming to be a developed country where equality prevails as for as gender is concerned, in reality still nourishes patriarchy. Rules are in text while society still upholds patriarchal notions where only a man be it a husband or a father has upper hand over matters of family and its members. Kidd shows this through her debut novel *The Secret Life of Bees* which is all about how the protagonist Lily struggles under her dominative father Terrance Ray whom everyone including the daughter calls as T.Ray. The novel in brief can be analysed as a journey that the neglected protagonist Lily Owens undertakes in her course of existence and the trauma both psychological and physical that she passes through.

The trauma studies or grief studies as mentioned earlier predominantly discourses on the loss of something and when it is a loss of human beings, the traumatic experiences get all the more tragic imparting untold miseries to those who grieve. Lily experiences this trauma of losing her mother at the very young age of four and it shatters her life beyond redemption. Adrienne Rich has rightly remarked that, "The loss of the … mother to the daughter, is the essential female tragedy" (qtd in Romero). Lily goes through this traumatic experiences at her younger age. The absence of mother affects her relationship with her father considerably. It is often a mother who builds a bond or a bridge between the father and child and when it is lost, the child loses some of the paternal affection too. This is very true of Lily. In the absence of the mother, the gender discordance between the father and the child aggravates.

Lily Owens was four when she lost her mother. The epigraph of the first chapter symbolically illustrates the state of a motherless house: "The queen, for her part, is the unifying force of the community; if she is removed from the hive, the workers very quickly sense her absence. After a few hours, or even less, they show unmistakable signs of queenlessness. – Man and Insects" (1). Lily is completely at a loss when she finds her father to be no caring and ignorant of a father's role. She learns what life is for a motherless daughter and that mother's love can never be matched or replaced by anybody else.

The loneliness and silence at home is too much for a small girl like Lily to put on and she longs for her mother. The mental trauma is so much that the little girl thinks about her death at the very early age. Lily recalls how, "That night I lay in bed and thought about dying and going to be with my mother in paradise" (1). She laments how the indignant father is very much attached to the pet dog Snout whom he does not admonish even if "Snout pee on T. Ray's boot and it not get a rise out of him" (4). Ironically, treating his dog with much greater affection than his own daughter, T.Ray continually devalues Lily by making her feel unloved. She earnestly prays, asking "God repeatedly to do something about T. Ray" (4). This behaviour speaks volumes about the mental agony that the girl is going through under the brutal behaviour of her father.

Like the bees that comes into her room, Lily feels listless, insecure, and unloved. Romero has rightly observed that

> When a daughter loses her mother, she loses the ally who will help her navigate the developmental challenges of life, form a secure sense of herself and her place in the world, and accept and survive the many losses which are an intrinsic part of living itself. She loses the witness who helped mark her passage through childhood, and the familiarity, recognition, and love which only a mother can provide. (Motherless Daughters 2017)

All these profound loses compel Lily to look for a way to escape from the suppressing ambience of her home.

When Lily becomes a teenager, her longing for her real mother Deborah intensifies. When she finds her mother's things, she makes up all kinds of stories about what her mother would have been like. Lily harbours romantic ideas about her mother and how she would have treated Lily if she were still alive brushing Lily's hair and teaching her about dating the boys. These are all kinds of events Lily pictures a mother doing for her emphasising mother's presence and wisdom.

The clothes she wears, her unkempt hair and the untidiness proclaim the trauma of a motherless child. It leads her to several unpleasant ramification in the matter of her appearance when she turns to fourteen years. The following passage unveils the anguish of a teenager who does not get the guidance and mending of a mother. She turns to her nanny Rosaleen in whom she tries to locate her mother. But she feels:

> Rosaleen knew less about fashion than T.Ray did, and when it was cold, God-help-me-Jesus, she made me go to school wearing long britches under my Pentecostal dresses. There was nothing I hated worse than clumps of whispering girls who got quiet when I passed. I started picking scabs off my body and, when I didn't have any, gnawing the flesh around my fingernails till I was a bleeding wreck. I worried so much about how I looked and whether I was doing things right, I felt half the time I was impersonating a girl instead of really being one. (8)

Her curly black hair due to the lack of care has turned into a nest of cowlicks. This unruly physical appearance affects Lily's confidence, and she starts to feel herself to be ugly. She worries about not having much of chin. Despite her lovely eyes and developing breasts, Lily confesses that even the hard-up boys give her no attention especially when she is forced to wear long britches under her Pentecostal dresses during the winter months. Her appearance causes her such anxiety that Lily takes to picking scabs of her body and chewing the flesh around her fingernails until she literally becomes bleeding wreck. She is so consumed with how she looks and whether she is behaving appropriately that she often feels like she is impersonating a girl instead of actually being one.

Lily undergoes untold mental anguishes due to the death of her mother. The final insult to Lily's motherless status is that she is denied entrance into charm school, which she believes would improve her appearance and manners because she has none to look after her. She laments "I had thought my real chance would come from going to charm school at the Women's club last spring, Friday afternoon for six weeks but I got barred because I didn't have a mother, a grandmother, or even a measly aunt to present me with a white rose at the closing ceremony. Rosaleen doing it was against the rules. I'd cried till I threw up in the sink" (8).

As Lily starts growing up, her grief also intensifies. She misses her mother on this journey which becomes all the more painful. She feels cast away and does not have any idea in matters "Like training bras. Who was I going to ask about that? And who but my mother could've understood the magnitude of driving me to junior cheerleader tryouts?" (11). And the worst part of her motherless status comes as in Lily's words thus: "But you know when I missed her the most? The day I was twelve and woke up with the rose-petal stain on my panties. I was so proud of that flower and didn't have a soul to show it to except Rosaleen" (11). These experiences proclaim the trauma of a teenager and how lost she must be feeling in the process of growing up.

Lily's state of insecurity and loneliness are aggravated by the lack of attention and love from the side of her only living parent, her father. He opens his mouth only to abuse the child and looks upon her as if she is a sworn-in enemy of him. This brutal upbringing makes the child incapable of loving him she confesses "My daddy –

who I called T. Ray because 'Daddy' never fit him" (3). This explains the strained relationship between the father and the daughter.

It is again the impact of trauma caused by the untimely death of his wife that turns T. Ray into a man of bitter temperament. T.Ray quite literally detests his daughter as she is the one who killed her mother accidently at the age of four. He overtly avoids her by working from sunup to sundown in the peach orchard. He is in no way interested in her physical or mental growth. His hatred goes a step ahead in thinking that education is a waste of money and time for a girl like her. The small girl already pining for the maternal love stands aghast at this paternal indifference.

T. Ray's cruelty amounts to even denying the girl the happiness of reading. In addition to his verbal and physical abuse, he also relishes in subjecting Lily to psychological abuse when he refuses to let her read while she works alone all day in the peach stand poster afraid it would start up ideas of college. To him, it is a waste of money for females to pursue higher education. Lily is an intelligent girl and even though she has scored the highest number a human being can possibly get on their Verbal Aptitude Test; T. Ray makes it sure that Lily never approaches him with an appeal of going to college. What the girl misses could be understood from the words of Mrs. Henry, Lily's teacher who tell her, "'Please, Lily, you are insulting your fine intelligence. Do you have any idea how smart you are? You could be a professor or a writer with actual books to your credit. Beauty school. Please.'" (12). Lily is very much aware of her potential and thereby knows how great her loss and she finds it difficult to come in terms with this reality and she confides, "It took me a month to get over the shock of having life possibilities. You know how adults love to ask, 'So…what are you going to be when you grow up?' I can't tell you how much I'd hated that question" (12).

Not only does T. Ray deny his daughter her right to education but forbids her from reading fearing it may equip her to challenge him and ask for better treatment. Kidd narrates how he abuses Lily once when he is been told that the girl was reading a book hiding it under her clothes. Seeing his anger Lily fears "he would half kill me. What kind of person is against reading? I think he believed it would stir up ideas of college, which he thought a waste of money for girls" (12).

Not only does the father denies his child education but he also robs the girl from even small and affordable pleasures of a teenager. He refuses to buy her rollers to fix the hair; He refuses to take her to football games, or any social function and he is unconcerned if she makes her own clothes and refuses to allow her wear more fashionable clothes. When she requests a silver charm bracelet for her 14th birthday, silence is his easy answer. He responds to her questions she asks about her mother with anger and violence, once by smashing a jar of blackberry preservers into the cabinet, leaving blue stains. His attempt at kindness in telling Lily the real story of what happened to her mother the day before the first grade quickly turns from kind awkwardness to anger when she tells him she remembers that they were arguing. He yells that she was only four and so she cannot possibly remember the details of that day.

The loss of mother itself is an incomparable loss to a child but the trauma she goes through at the thought of she being the cause of it totally shatters Lily. When her father talks of the day she accidently shot her mother: "For a moment everything got still and quiet, as if the wind had died and the birds had stopped flying. When he squatted down in front of me, I felt caught in a hot dark I could not break free of" (13). Later, he softens when he tells her that she did not mean to do it, but this is as much kindness as Lily can expect. The trauma she has been undergoing as a motherless child flashes across her mind. She recalls how despite her overwhelming need for love and affirmation in the years following her mother's death, T.Ray is an emotionally absent father but consistent in verbally abusing in all of their interactions.

Lily remembers the night when excited by the bee swarming in her room, wakes him up to show him the phenomenon, he angrily responds "'Goddamn it, Lily, this ain't funny.'" and when he sees no bees he threatens "You wake me up again, Lily, and I'll get out the Martha Whites, you hear me?' Martha Whites were a form of punishment only T. Ray could have dreamed up. I shut my mouth instantly" (5).

Physical and verbal abuse are quite common in Lily's life as she is constantly exposed to them right from her childhood. It does not lessen even when she grows into a teenager. Two nights before her fourteenth birthday, she is in the peach orchard holding close to her chest some precious keepsakes of her mother's in order to feel closer to her mother. T.Ray finds her in the middle of the night putting up her shirt. Believing her to have been with the boy, his menacing anger erupts as he tells her

> 'I expect this out of boys, Lily – you can't blame them – but I expect more out of you. You act no better than a slut'. He poured a mound of grits the size of an anthill onto the pine floor. 'Get over here and kneel down. 'I'd been kneeling on grits since I was six, but still I never got used to that powdered-glass feeling beneath my skin. I walked toward them with those tiny feather steps you expect of a girl in Japan, and lowered myself to the floor, determined not to cry, but the sting was already gathering in my eyes. T. Ray sat in a chair and cleaned his nails with a pocketknife. I swayed from knee to knee, hoping for a second or two of relief, but the pain cut deep into my skin. I bit down on my lip, and it was then I felt the wooden picture of black Mary underneath my waistband. I felt the waxed paper with my mother's picture inside and her gloves stuck to my belly, and it seemed all of a sudden like my mother was there, up against my body, like she was bits and pieces of insulation molded against my skin, helping me absorb all his meanness. (18)

The brutal punishment makes Lily sick and as a result wakes up little late the next morning. This angers T. Ray more and Lily is finally convinced that any love T.Ray has for her so far is gone when she takes her slice of buttered bread, he grabs it from her and throws it into the dog's bowl and scolds her for starting work late. He continuously devalues her, making her feel unwanted and unloved.

Research shows how such feelings of unwantedness, and lack of love makes the children rebellious, and they gain the courage to step out from the safety of their home. They "feel that running away is the only solution not to face the embarrassment. In addition to that, fear, failure or anger are other reasons that make teens run away from home. Some children find it difficult to adjust to their family members or critical home situation and think to escape out" (Saha Mom Junction). Lily undergoes fear, embarrassment of being abused, identifies oneself as a bad girl with no sense of belonging in her own home. Hence, when the conditions worsen at home and when she feels strangled and suffocated, Lily escapes with her nanny Rosaleen. She seeks refuge in the Boatwright sisters who satisfy her longing for mother to some extent. Though racial barriers are there, the refined love helps her cross her racial prejudice and feels safe under the loving hands of August and Rosaleen. It is there, Lily develops confidence and identity. There is a progress in her psychic development, she learns to bee-keeping under August's training and thus evolves into self-supporting youngster. The confidence helps her to overcome the trauma of her childhood and find a purpose of her existence.

Despite Lily's relief about being loved by so many people in the pink house of Boatwright sisters, the discovery that the idealised Debora Owens she has so long embraced was not a truth and that her mother had left both her and her father because she was unable to cope with T.Ray anymore shatters her. This knowledge devastates Lily to the point that she quite literally has a meltdown in the honey-house later on smashing jars of honey against the walls and injuring her arm faster. The knowledge means that both of the parents ultimately rejected her. This means that Lily can no longer entertain the smug of delusion that her life would have been much better if her mother was still alive. Soon she understands that she will have to forgive her mother if she wants to continue moving forward faster

Kidd proves through her debut novel that the effective way to release a mind from the mental trauma is to forget the pain and forgive those who cause it. Lily learns this great lesson at her younger age. The realisation dawns on her after reading Blake's poem from the books collection of her mother, Lily realises that she was one of the reasons that her mother had died. Her mother had not planned to marry T.Ray, but when she became pregnant with Lily, she decided to marry him. Lily desperately wants to apologise to her mother when she sees a picture which eases her troubled mind from the feeling of abandonment. Her mother had framed a picture of herself feeding Lily in a highchair. Lily explains that now she did not care about anything on this earth except the way her mother's face was tipped towards hers, their noses just touching, how wide and gorgeous her mother's smile was, like sparklers going off. The picture is an actual proof that Deborah Owens had loved her daughter, and finally Lily feels loved by her mother. Now that she has all the facts, Lily has only to forgive her mother for leaving her. She kept thinking how nobody is perfect and that one has to let the puzzle of the human heart be what it is. So, she completely understands her mother's decision to leave, and now she is ready to forgive her. This psychologically releases her from the mental trauma and an idol of black Mary which August gives strengthens Lily from within. August advises her to seek support from it whenever she feels dejected and disappointed. It helps Lily considerably to overcome her grief and relieves her psychologically from the feeling of being cast away.

The spiritual power equips Lily even to forgive her father who traces her whereabout and arrives at the doorstep of August. When T.Ray sees the whale pin on Lily's shirt which belonged to his wife

Deborah, his chin quivers and for the first time Lily realises how much her father must have loved her mother:

> The thought seemed to awe him. He shook his head and looked around, as if thinking, I bet she sat in this chair. I bet she walked on this rug. His chin quivered slightly, and for the first time it hit me how much he must've loved her, how it had split him open when she left. Before coming here, my whole life had been nothing but a hole where my mother should have been, and this hole had made me different, left me always aching for something, but never once did I think what he'd lost or how it might've changed him. (205)

The months of nurturing at the pink house of Boatwright sisters allows her to see beyond her own suffering, Lily could see T.Ray's weakness. He is no longer the bitter abusive father who makes Lily kneel on grits. He is a broken man trying to face the fact that he had caused both his wife and his daughter to run away from him. He permits Lily to stay with August where she is allowed to study and engage in bee keeping too.

Thus, the novel though traces the traumatic experiences of a motherless girl who is also deprived of father's love, ends on a positive note. It shows how the unfortunate girl finally wins the selfless love of mother Mary in addition to the love of mothers like August, her sisters and her nanny Rosaleen. She avers, "All these mothers. I have more mothers than any eight girls off the street. They are the moons shining over me" (211). For a fourteen-year-old high school student who has learned to forgive her imperfect parents, embrace the love of a host of black women is indeed remarkable and this exemplary quality redeems her from the trauma of dejected love she has been suffering from her childhood.

Works Cited

Balaev, Michelle. "Trends in Literary Trauma Theory." Mosaic (Winnipeg) 41.2 (June 2008): 149. *Literature Resource Center*. Accessed 26 Jan. 2011.

Kidd, Sue Monk. *The Secret Life of Bees*. Headline Book,2002. (z-lib.org).epub.pdf. 2 August 2021.

Romero, Rawna Chery. *Motherless Daughters*. 28 Jan. 2017. Accessed 5 August 2021.

Saha, Ria. "Why Do Teens Run Away and How to Deal With It?" *Mom Junction*. June 8, 2021. Accessed 8 August 2021

CHAPTER 2

Transcending the Collective Trauma of 9/11: Susan L. Roth's *It's Still a Dog's New York: A Book of Healing*

Dr. Manju R.

"But then on September 11, 2001 something so huge and horrible happened that the whole world shook." (Kalman, 2002, p.23). The September 11,2001 terrorist attacks were one of the deadliest terrorist acts ever to occur in the United States and these were unprecedented in terms of their scope and traumatic impact on the American psyche. The attacks on World Trade Center and the Pentagon have set a new context for deliberations on the concept of collective trauma. When large segments of population, have to bear the impact of either natural or human – caused adversities, it becomes a collective trauma. As Smelser (2004) writes, 9/11 was a complicated moment, an "ambivalent event-simultaneously shocking and fascinating, depressing and exhilarating, grotesque and beautiful…and leaving the country feeling both bad and good about itself" (p.269). According to Maurice Saxby, children's books "perhaps more than any other print media reflect social change" (p.416). The books written about major critical events is an important source of new and competing discourses with respect to identity, culture, race and citizenship. A study of children's books about 9/11 is significant in understanding how identities emerge and compete in the stories.

Susan L. Roth is the author/illustrator of 45 books for children. She uses collage as her primary medium and she illustrates her tales with cut and torn papers, threads, fabrics and wood-cuts. In her picture book, *It's Still a Dog's New York: A Book of Healing* (2001), two American dogs grieve over what has happened to their city and find hope and strength through revisiting New York's most iconic sites.

As they do this, they give the readers a sanctioned version of New York and cook up a strengthened identity for New Yorkers.

Many theorists, including G. Ray, (2005) have claimed that traumatic national events have often resulted in periods of time when national identity takes priority over other identifications. The significance of memory and forgetfulness in forming a post-9/11 identity is evident on the cover of the book which illustrates the two dogs, Rover and Pepper leaning against buildings.

Figure 1 It's a Dog's New York (Cover)

Figure 2 It's Still a Dog's New York : A Book of Healing (Cover)

The picture book, *It's Still a Dog's New York: A Book of Healing* is a sequel to the author's original *It's a Dog's New York* (2001). Roth had just finished the first book when the tragic events of September 11 occurred. Being a person born in America and settled in New York, she felt sorry for the plight of the children of New York City. She wanted to address the fears, doubts and anxieties that youngsters might have about the horrible events. So, she created a smaller version of the original, rewriting the text and slightly changing the title. In the post 9/11 sequel, the word "still" is inserted into the title with '^'. The author seems to suggest that it is the same New York, yet different. The dogs in both the books are dressed as the Statue of Liberty. But in the post 9/11 sequel, they are waving their national flags. The cover of the book symbolises the resurgence of patriotic spirit following a national crisis. It is also a reminder that the nation still upholds the values of truth, justice and liberty.

The construction of a romantic past is one of the strategies used in the book to convince citizens that they have a personal national responsibility. Though the Twin Towers acquired symbolic significance after 9/11, this book firmly etches them into our memories as though they had always been symbolically this significant. When Rover asks, "remember where the World Trade Center was?" and Pepper retorts, "those two towers are still in my head as …plain as day!" (p.22), a particular iconic image is evoked. Though a young reader may never have seen the Twin Towers, he or she is encouraged to behave as though he or she has seen it.

Memory is a recurrent discourse in the book. The author seems to suggest that remembering and telling one's story is essential for a healthy recovery from trauma. The book remembers the New York that was, and although it makes reference to 9/11 throughout, both the illustrations and the print text create a collective memory of a romanticised, innocent pre-9/11 New York. The trauma is erased as Pepper and Rover remember and embrace what New York was prior to the attack. As Jo Lampert comments, "the book, in effect, is about getting those memories back, valuing what was, what still "is" and moving on from 9/11" (97).

The spirit of optimism reigns supreme in the book. Americans, after a short, but poignant period of despair, are reinstated as being assertive, confident, and able to move on. Pepper is always sentimental and desperate over the traumatic incident, but Rover, the bigger dog consistently takes on the responsibility of turning this despair around. When Pepper says, "there is nothing to celebrate now," Rover retorts, "so many brave heroes came to our rescue … believe me Pepper, that's something to celebrate!" (p.18). He empathises with Pepper's fears, but argues her out of them: "I feel this way, too, but we have to go on" (p.4). "We'll have to try very hard, but it's still a dog's New York!" (p.20). He also emphasizes the need to work together for a common cause: "We'll get through this if we work hard together" (p.24). "These are hard times for America…But we're strong" (p.23). The relationship between Pepper and Rover rewrites 9/11 so that, hopefulness and optimism are ingrained as national characteristics.

In the book, New York City functions not merely as backdrop, but it becomes the central element in the reshaping of a national identity. With its photographic collages, images of the gloriously remembered New York City are hammered home until they are deeply embedded in the reader's memories. One illustration includes idyllic repeated images of an imagined Central Park replete with trees, skaters, horses and New Yorkers with their pets (p.8). However, it is a sanitized, artificial and romantic picture of the city that we get from the book. There is no evidence of the homelessness, racial tension or crime that are also recurrent themes in New York narratives. The dogs visit libraries, museums, concert halls and Times Square. The places visited are historic landmarks, evoking a belief in shared history. It imagines that all New Yorkers demonstrate these high-cultured interests, pursuits and sources of knowledge.

Americans are represented in this book as naturally and collectively heroic. They are compelled to behave in a manner that is both caring and forceful and powerful and peaceful. Pepper says, "We can roar like the lions against the horrible things that happened. We can roar like lions for peace" (p.104). This contradictory response, making the use of force appear gentle was strategic after 9/11.Despite the horrible happenings, the dogs, who are representatives of the American public have faith that the nations' leaders can be trusted to keep their citizens safe. Rover tells Pepper, "Don't worry. Big dogs are working twenty-four hours a day to make us safe" (p.10).

In spite of the reassuring images within the text that the Americans are strong, secure and safe, almost every illustration in the book is broken up by a band of colour. This can be taken as a symbol of broken and fragmented America. However, in the narrative progression of the illustrations, an order is returned and the location is re-secured. On the second last page of the book, the photographs of buildings are straight and tall rather than jumbled and disorderly. The last page of the book provides a map of New York City. The brave American is re-located and reminded that he / she can once again find his / her way around. Another interesting illustration used is that of paper cranes-symbols of peace-flying around the Empire State Building. The use of this image is complicated by the fact that the atomic bombs were dropped in Hiroshima and Nagasaki by America. The use of this symbol can be read both as an admission of guilt and as an opportunity to erase that guilt by claiming a moral comparison.

The pedagogical intent in this book, as in most of the books written for children, is explicit. The dedication in this book proclaims its desire to tell children "who to be". A statement on the cover page of the book explains that the author has taken advice from three child psychiatrists who made sure that the book speaks, as it should, to children. This statement gives the readers a clue as to how the book should be read-as a prescription to heal a nation. In representing the national identity, the notion of a "healing" nation takes centrality. America is represented as capable of being hurt, vulnerable and in need of healing, despite a tough core.

American history is re-told, rewritten and narrated in this book. The dogs, Rover and Pepper can be read as representatives of the national collective. The book provides a blue print for who we should be in such times of crisis, how we should behave, feel and think about what has happened and about our futures. America is ordered to demonstrate a collective goal and community strength. Thus, *It's Still a Dog's New York: A Book of Healing,* functions as a post-9/11 narrative by attempting to heal the traumatised minds of children of New York City and instilling in them the spirit of optimism and courage to move on with their lives.

Works Cited

Kalman, M. *Fireboat: The Heroic Adventures of John J.* Harvcy. New York: G.P.Putnam's Sons, 2002.

Lampert, Jo. *Children's Fiction about 9/11.* New York: Routledge, 2010.

Ray, G. *Terror and Sublime in Art and Critical Theory: From Auschwitz to Hiroshima to September 11.* New York: Palgrave Macmillan, 2005.

Roth, Susan L. *It's Still a Dog's New York: A Book of Healing.* Washington D.C.: National Geographic Society, 2001.

Saxby, Maurice. *The Proof of the Pudding: Australian Children's Literature 1970-1990.* Sydney: Ashton Scholastic, 1993.

Smelser, N.J. *Cultural Trauma and Collective Identity.* Berkeley: University of California Press, 2004.

CHAPTER 3

Quest of the Traumatised Self: A Revelation of Emigrant Issues

Soubhagya S.P. and Dr. N.U. Lekshmi

Indian Literature in English has a prominent place among World Literature and it expresses a shared tradition, cultural experience and Indian heritage. Translation plays a significant role in the enrichment of Indian English literature. There are a number of regional languages in India and a wide variety of writings are being produced in great number in these regional languages reflecting the diverse aspects of Indian society. Translation remains as an integral part of Indian literary life and according to the famous Malayalam writer K. Satchidanandan "Translation for us today is a way of retrieving our people's histories and recording their past and present" (qtd.in Dennis Abrams). Translation is opening a new chapter in Malayalam literary arena and nowadays almost all the works written in Malayalam are being translated into English and this gives Malayalam literature a particular space among the World Literature. The translation had helped Malayalam literature to break away from the confinement within a smaller range of audience and brought it to the mainstream literature. Translation of Malayalam fiction into English places Malayalam literature in the national and international contexts. There are a large number of writers who had attained universal fame through their translated works.

Benyamin is a significant figure in the Malayalam literary arena and almost all his works written in Malayalam had been translated into English. He makes use of his writings to portray the struggles faced by emigrants in the gulf countries. Benyamin's *Goat Days* is a heart wrenching narrative of the haunting experiences of Najeeb as a slave in the gulf country. The novel is written in Malayalam as *Aadujeevitham* and it was later translated into English by Joseph Koyippally. The book is based on the real life incidents of a person named Najeeb in the desert land and after listening to the horrific experiences underwent by Najeeb, the author felt the urge to write it down as to showcase to the world the physical and psychic trauma encountered by Najeeb as a slave in an unfamiliar world without the companionship of any other human being except his master. The book published in 2008 had also won the prestigious Kerala Sahitya Academy award. The book chronicles the harrowing experiences of Najeeb, a Keralite who always nurtured the hope to migrate to gulf as to improve the life conditions. But all his dreams about gulf were so much distant from the harsh reality that he endured for three years in the desert land amidst complete loneliness. Instead of the job offer he expected, he was forced to work under an abusive Arbab (master) who treated him very badly. Unlike his homeland, the water and food were provided scarcely to Najeeb and that made his life much tougher. Najeeb was a man who worked as a sand miner in his land and much of his time was spent in water. So that in the beginning days of his stay in the desert, he felt very hard to live without water. Gradually he accustoms himself to the lesser use of water mainly to escape from the cruel beatings of his Arbab and also as part of his survival. According to Existentialists:

> Existence... is a constant *striving*, a perpetual *choice*; it is marked by a radical freedom and *responsibility*; and it is always prey to a sense of *Angst* which reveals that, for the most part, it lived *inauthenticity* and in *bad faith*. And because the character of a human life is never *given*, existence is without foundation; hence it is abandoned or even absurd. (6)

Survival attains high significance in the novel as it chronicles the struggles encountered by Najeeb to survive in a land very much alien to him. Najeeb had always wished for the opportunity to work in gulf country as to have a better life so that when he got a visa he was very happy to go there. Najeeb yearned to work in the gulf country very much that he describes it as the "city of my dreams" (43). But all his dreams about his new life shattered all of a sudden when the Arbab took him to the Masara (goat shed) in the middle of the desert. From there onwards he was forced to live a life entirely alienated from other people under the savage attitude of his Arbab. In the beginning Najeeb found it very hard to accept the reality that he was trapped in the middle of the desert without the companionship of any other human beings except his Arbab who opened his mouth only to abuse Najeeb. Slowly Najeeb adapted himself to the reality that he started leading his life by herding the goats and looking after the sheep and camels.

The novel is an engaging tale of survival that, inspite of the harsh treatment that he received from his arbab, Najeeb always hoped for an escape from that cruel world to a life with his family in homeland. Trauma of being alone hits him hard. Cathy Caruth in the work *Unclaimed Experience: Trauma, Narrative and History* defines trauma as "the response to an unexpected or overwhelming violent event or events that are fully grasped as they occur, but return later in repeated flash-backs, nightmares and other repetitive phenomenon" (91). He acculturates himself with the life condition in the Masara that he became one and the same with the goats. He develops a close attachment with goats as to develop his survival instincts. He develops a companionship with them so that he could talk to them about his pains and longings. It is this companionship that helps him to hang on to his life in the desert land for three years, four months, nine days. The animals in the Masara which include goats, camels and sheep were the constant companions of Najeeb throughout his stay in that land. Najeeb's life as a slave proves that circumstances make a man capable of learning to do anything. Najeeb who had never touched a goat in his lifetime was forced to spend his life among a large number of goats by herding and milking them. Even though he developed the skill of herding goats and milking them as part of his survival and as a way to escape from the cruel beatings of the Arbab, gradually he becomes so much attached to the goats. When in the end he along with Hakeem and Ibrahim Khadiri came up with a way to escape from the Masara, Najeeb found it very hard to bid farewell to his goats with whom he shared all his sufferings.

The animals in the Masara were the most critical factors that helped Najeeb to survive in that strange land. He used to confide all his pains and longings to the goats and in a way this helped him to reduce his sufferings. He used to talk to them whenever possible and he poured out his "tears, pains, sufferings, emotions and dreams" (168). He doesn't know whether they had understood his language and his emotions but he felt so much comfort and solace after pouring out all his pains and sorrows. He used to give names to the goats in the Masara as to recognise them easily and this also developed his intimacy with the goats. He named the goats in association with the people from his homeland such as Aravu Ravuthar, Mary Maimuna, Pinki, Ammu and sometimes he named them in association with the public figures like Jagathy and Mohanlal. He says:

> Each of them was dear to me in one way or another. Have you ever looked carefully at a goat's face? It is quite similar to human's. I named the goats not only by looking at their faces but also relating their names to some character traits, their gait, and the sounds they made by incidents that reminded me of them. Just as how one gets a nickname back home. (161)

There was a particular goat with which Najeeb was so much attached that the goat had played a crucial role in improvising Najeeb's craving for survival. He named the goat as Nabeel after his son whom he had not seen yet. Najeeb's wife Sainu was pregnant when he left the country and after reaching the Masara, Najeeb lost contact with the world around him that he was unable to connect even with his family. He was ignorant of any information regarding his wife or child. It is at this painful situation that one of the goats in the Masara delivered a male goat that too in Najeeb's hands. He believed that it was a good omen from God's part to help him get over all the struggles that he endures. He says: "Maybe this was a good omen Allah wanted to show me. My Sainu, my wife--- she has given birth. A baby boy, as I had longed for. In that belief, I named that new-born goat Nabeel. The name I had thought of for my son" (107). The goat Nabeel was a source of comfort in the desolated life of Najeeb. In the extremely harsh life in the desert, Najeeb was in need of something to hold on to survive and Nabeel acted as a source of hope for Najeeb to escape from that strange land.

Najeeb always longed to escape from the cruel hands of his Arbab but at the same time he was so patient that he never rushed when opportunities came. For him, his life is precious, he says: "I didn't have enough food, water, clothes, a proper place to sleep, wages, dreams or aspirations. But I did have something very precious left- my life! I had at least managed to sustain that" (141). Even though he wished deeply to escape from the Masara he waited patiently for the apt time so that he could enjoy freedom at its best. And at this long term of waiting for the right time to escape, Najeeb learnt to adapt himself to the life in desert familiarising himself with the routines of his Arbab as well as with that of the animals in the Masara. Everything in that land is new for him: the Arbab, the gun, the language, the Masara, the Khubus, the goats, the camels, the desert, the climate, his job and so many other things in that land. Yet he adapts himself to the situations in that land.

Another factor that added to strengthen Najeeb's struggle for survival under the Arbab is his constant faith in God. Even in his extreme agony he didn't gave up his belief in the power of Allah, the supreme power. He had always believed that God will offer him something more beautiful in return to all the hardships that he endured throughout his stay in the desert. It is his faith in the supreme power that instilled his confidence and he tells: "For me, prayers were my bolt-hole. It was because of faith alone that I could be strong in spirit even when I was weak in my body. Otherwise I would have withered and burnt like grass in that blazing wind" (153). Najeeb was a strong believer in the power of God that it helped him in his desolate life as a slave in the desert.

Even though Najeeb had always nurtured the hope to escape from his harrowing life in Masara, on the other hand he adapted himself to the harsh reality which he was experiencing. Along with his struggle for survival, he had also learnt to live with his circumstances. As the time passes, one becomes used to the daily routine of his life and so Najeeb also became accustomed to the life of a slave amidst the goats and his life was no more troublesome for him. And in the end as he hoped God offered him help in the form of Ibrahim Khadiri who helped Najeeb to escape from the cruel clutches of his Arbab. The theme of survival plays a significant role in the novel *Goat Days* by Benyamin as it showcases the traumatic experiences that Najeeb was forced to undergo in a Masara in the middle of the desert under the harsh treatment of his Arbab. Najeeb faces extreme severity in the desert both by the climatic conditions as well as by the cruel treatments of his Arbab. Yet he struggles extremely to survive from all the traumatic experiences and nurtures the hope for escape. The severe life situations could not diminish Najeeb's strength of mind. It is strong will to endure all the hardships that made him escape from the desolate life which he was forced to lead. Benyamin through the portrayal of Najeeb showcases to the world the harsh reality that was experienced by people like Najeeb in gulf countries and also emphasises how strong will and mental power could help a man to survive all the hardships.

Works Cited

Benyamin. *Goat Days.* Translated by Joseph Koyippally. Penguin publishers. 2012.

Caruth, Cathy. *Unclaimed Experience: Trauma, Narrative and History.* Hopkins UP, 1996.

Abrams, Dennis. "Why Translation is Integral to Indian Literary Life." *Publishing Perspectives.*2Dec.2013.<http://www.publishingperspectives.com//> 15 Oct. 2017

Waheed, S. C. "Literature in the Oil Age: A Review of Goat Days". *Chapati Mystery.* 11 Jan 2016, <http:/www.chapatimystery.com>

CHAPTER 4

Rising Like a Phoenix: Narratives on Acid Attack in India

Asha P. V.

Trauma studies deal with the impact of trauma in different facets of human experience. If proper care is not given to trauma victims, it can shatter their identity very badly. Traumatic experience can exert a negative influence and persist as a ghostlike presence throughout the person's life. So utmost care must be given to people who faced traumatic experiences, moreover post-traumatic stress disorder also needs to be checked thoroughly. Post-traumatic stress disorder develops as a result of exposure to a life threatening situation or experience. Trauma affects not only the person but also those around. Narratives of traumatic experience can have a cathartic effect and it is important to give vent to the experience. Trauma narratives help to make sense of the unexplainable emotion the victims go through. Trauma can occur for a myriad number of reasons; it can be physical trauma or psychological trauma. Narratives on acid attack can come under both physical and psychological trauma. Acid attack is one of the most disgusting and cruelest forms of attack a person can inflict on another person. In most of the cases women and children are the victims of this heinous crime, but one should not forget that men also come under attack in some cases. The use of acid as a weapon began to rise in many developing nations, specifically in South Asia. Since acid can be easily purchased in these countries and is relatively cheap as compared to other weapons like guns, it was a preferred weapon. The first recorded acid attack occurred in India in 1982 (Zalmai 13). Acid attack causes not just physical deformities but also deep psychological and mental trauma.

If we analyse the reasons behind such crimes, one find that rejection in love, family issues, dowry related issues, sexual tension etc. are the common causes. Acid attacks are often referred to "as a 'crime of passion,' fuelled by the refusal of romantic and sexual advances, jealousy and revenge" (Bhullar). When the ego of men gets hurt, they react in horrifying ways; it happens mainly because they cannot face rejection. Men think that they can dominate over women by causing them lifelong trauma. The patriarchal society of our country considers acid attack as a medium to suppress women. United Nations Organisation characterises violence as, "any demonstration of brutality that outcomes in or is probably going to bring about physical, sexual or mental damage or enduring to an individual including danger of such act lasting or temporary deprivation of freedom whether happening in the general population or private life" (UN 1993).

Acid attack has devastating effect on health. Acid burns through skin and flesh and no one can bear the excruciating pain and trauma. Strong acids can even dissolve metals, so think about the effect it can have on a mere human body. That thought itself is disgusting and horrifying. From an Indian perspective, "noting that stigma, patriarchy, misogyny and weak legislation contribute to acid attack incidents" (Winter 75). Acid attack is pure violence. "Disfigured, distorted and shamed for no fault of theirs, victims of acid attacks have many a fight on their hands- trauma, a cold hearted society and sluggish judicial system to name a few" (*India Today* 1). Narratives on acid attack have played a major role in opening up the turmoil the victims and their family go through. These are not just any ordinary narratives of pain, because the PAIN (author's own emphasis) and shame they feel is beyond words can describe.

Reshma Qureshi is an acid attack survivor and she has published her autobiography *Being Reshma: The Extraordinary Story of an Acid-Attack Survivor Who Took the World by Storm* (2018) along with Tania Singh. She was attacked by her brother-in-law when she was just seventeen. In this work she tears open the double standard of Indian society and tells the readers what it means to live with scars in India. She states,

> The point is that acid-attack survivors in India are shamed. We live in a culture of victim-blaming. Many of us never leave our homes because of the hostile stares, gestures, comments directed at us, and because of how differently we are treated from everyone else. Only a handful of us ever find jobs, and even if some of us do, it is in government-sanctioned projects that require us to be hired under quotas. (243)

Victim blaming is rampant in India especially if the victim is a woman. Reshma Qureshi talks at length about the deep trauma it caused to her and her parents. Her elder sister's husband Jamaluddin threw acid at her when she was just seventeen years old. Reshma's sister Gulshan was married to Jamaluddin and she faced severe domestic violence and abuses at his home. Finally Reshma's family decided to keep their daughter with them, but things take a violent turn when he decided to revenge upon Gulshan. Jamaluddin thought he threw the acid on his wife's face but it was actually Reshma who was caught in the middle of all these because she was wearing her sister's niqab. It requires a brave heart to read her trauma and the pain she endures. The antipathy of society, mistreatment of hospital staff and doctors added to her misery. Even the police was not helping them. Her mother has to describe the whole incident to everyone again and again to get proper treatment to Reshma, but even then for the hospital authorities she was just a patient with a 'disease'. "Acid is a corrosive substance that continues to burn even hours after the person has been attacked with it. The only way to minimize the damage is to flush the affected area for hours with water. Water dilutes the acid. No nurse or doctor made this suggestion" (92). If they had acted fast she could have avoided so many surgeries and operations. The authorities were insisting on getting an FIR copy before starting her treatment. She narrates the tragedy thus:

> I was in excruciating pain because for me, it was not just my skin burning but my soul too. I was shouting as loudly as I could to tell them everything that had happened. By this time, it was more than seven hours since the attack and I had still not received treatment. That's how I lost vision in my left eye. My family was broken. My father was running around to arrange for money for my treatment and multiple surgeries. We even had to sell all our property to pay for the treatment. (90)

Justice delayed is justice denied, and in her case she is delayed justice and treatment. Immediate treatment should be given to them without waiting for the official formalities. She faced depression, and post-traumatic stress disorder. She even thought of putting an end to her life several times because of the excruciating physical and mental pain. The non-acceptance of society causes deep mental traumas for the survivors and if proper care is not given to them, they may put an end to their life because suicidal tendencies are very high among this group. Slow judicial processes and inadequate compensation only add up to the worries of acid attack survivors.

She talks at length about the reaction of the people who witnessed the heinous crime. "Those narrow streets with over a hundred people bore witness to my pain, but no one had the courage or the will to stop my attackers as they fled. I can't even blame them because I believe they were truly afraid" (86). What Reshma portrays is a very typical Indian attitude. Unless the people they know are in danger, they will not even raise a finger at the issue. "After the show was over, they turned their backs on me, the way I imagine they ignore injured stray animals every day" (87). The same crowd later looks at her with contempt; it is difficult to get mercy from people. Some even went to the extreme of blaming her for instigating the crime.

Her life gets a new direction and meaning when she met Ria Sharma, the founder of Make Love Not Scars. The organisation works on the rehabilitation of acid attack survivors providing them with financial aid and also emotional and psychological support. Rehabilitation and after care is of utmost importance to the acid attack survivors.

Disfiguring a woman's body is seen as an end to her life in a patriarchal society like India. Because beauty is seen as a parameter for women's success, by disfiguring the body, the culprits think that they have successfully destroyed her. Perpetrators want to destroy the beauty of women because in Indian society people give undue importance to the physical appearance of women. Acid victims had to face oppositions from social media sites while posting their pictures, "On many occasions, social media sites such as Facebook, have removed photographs and videos of survivors because someone would flag certain content as 'graphic' and report it" (202). Disfiguring of bodies is a common issue faced by them. They are not allowed to present their reality just because it is offensive to some.

What patriarchy forgets is that beauty is not being fair or having clean skin. Naomi Wolf in *The Beauty Myth* says that "the rise of the beauty myth was just one of several emerging social fictions that masqueraded as senatural components of the feminine sphere, the better to enclose those women inside it." Reshma Qureshi is a beautiful girl even after the acid attack simply because her beauty emanates from inside not outside.

Reshma became the worldwide face of #endacidsale campaign and also the first acid attack survivor to walk the runway at the New York Fashion Week. This walk is now part of history. Reshma gave small beauty tutorials and it instantly caught the attention of everyone. "The campaign was launched on The Logical Indian on August 30, 2015. Each vlog ended with a plea to crowd source signatures on a petition addressed to the Prime Minister for enforcing the ban on open sale of acid" (Best Media Info). Now she is in peace with her life because the acid has only left scars in her face not her mind. The campaign was hard hitting with among the masses and it snowballed into a request to stop acid sale. In 2013 the Supreme Court has banned the over-the-counter-sale of acids in India. But the sad fact is that even now acid is available in markets for sale despite judicial interventions. Advocate Prashant Kumar said, "Making a law is useless until it is implemented in its true spirit. Similar is for implementation of court directives. Our state is trying to tackle the problem of acid attack, so law enforcing agencies, especially police and intelligence, will have to be very strict" (Hindustan Times). As per the guidelines, the shop and seller must have a valid license and they must keep a record of the people who come to buy acids. But it is not put into practice in most cases.

"In 2014, the United Nations described violence against women in India as a systematic crime that stretches 'from the womb to the tomb'" (Wahab 1). India has the highest number of acid attacks in the world. "Figures released by the National Crime Records Bureau (NCRB) found that between 2014 and 2018, there have been nearly 1,500 victims of acid attacks in the country" (Krishnan 6). When we deal with acid attack survivors, care must be given to ensure a holistic approach which covers every facets of their conditions. Reshma Qureshi is not a victim, but a survivor. Reshma gained strength "from knowing that my attacker wanted to "ruin" my life and I would get the sweetest revenge by living an accomplished, successful and happy life" (Bisht). She flies like a phoenix in this world fighting against all odds. In an interview, Reshma gives the reason why she writes about her journey. "By putting a face to acid violence through my journey, I wish to inspire those who are stuck in violent, abusive relationships, those who need to know about the harsh reality we face as women in India, those who wish to bring about change, yet don't know how, those who just wish to know more about acid attacks and most importantly, those who feel as though they can't overcome their current obstacles" (Bisht)

Acid narratives have caught the attention of filmmakers too. Films have the potential in creating an intense level of empathy towards the characters on screen. In 2019 Manu Ashokan made his directorial debut with the film *Uyare*, which portrays the trials and tribulations of the protagonist Pallavi Raveendran. Pallavi is an aviation student where good looks matter a lot. The conventional idea of beauty which is based entirely on skin colour and looks, is very regressive. Real beauty lies in a person's character and behavior. Pallavi's obsessive boyfriend Govind throws acid at her when she decided to end her toxic relationship with him. But she is saved from despair by her strong support system. Though the film suffers from predictability the directo, it is able to bring the best of all the characters and sensitively portrays the nuances of the story. So many films and other mediums are taking up their cause. Some try to make a sensation and some others trivialise the issue but what they forget is that acid attack is one of the most horrific accidents. The 2020 Bollywood movie *Chhapaak* narrates the life of Laxmi Agarwal, an acid attack survivor. Deepika Padukone portrays her character on screen. These films are not easy to watch but it tears open society's prejudices and lays bare the life of an acid attack survivor.

Trauma is not an easy concept to elucidate because of its different kinds of manifestations in different people. We have a history of repressing the unspeakable and it requires immense courage to actually speak. The trope of the unspeakable acquires new dimensions with the trauma theory. Various forms of violences lead to trauma especially violences like acid attack which causes long term post-traumatic stress disorder. The pain interferes in their daily actions. According to Nguyen, out of the 1500 total cases reported globally every year, approximately 1000 are committed in India. The Convention on the Elimination of All Forms of Discrimination Against Women defines gender-based violence as, "violence directed against women because she is a woman or which affects a woman disproportionately" (2). It includes physical, mental, emotional or sexual harm or sufferings.

To eradicate acid violence, governments must address its root causes: "gender inequality and discrimination, the availability of acid, and the impunity of perpetrators... Enact criminal laws that specifically address acid violence and effectively regulate the production, distribution, use, sale, and handling of acid; Effectively enforce and implement laws designed to deter acid violence; and Provide victim redress, including compensation for healthcare costs" (Kalantry 1). Bangladesh enforces strict laws to curtail acid attack by introducing death penalty for the attackers. But even death penalty is not an adequate punishment for the culprits. The government and judiciary should make sure the laws are implemented rightly; otherwise no one can put an end to these man-made miseries.

Works Cited

Best Media Info Bureau. *Reshma Qureshi makes a powerful case for ending sale of acid.* 16 Sept. 2015. bestmediainfo.com/2015/09/reshma-qureshi-makes-a-powerful-case-for-ending-sale-of-acid/. Accessed 14 Aug. 2021.

Bhullar, D.S. *Acid throwing: A cause of concern. Journal of Punjab Academy of Forensic Medicine* & *Toxicology*, vol. 13, no. 2, 2014, pp. 60-62. Accessed 2 Aug. 2021.

Bisht, Bhawana. *My Book Aims To Empower All Those Who Face Abuse: Reshma Qureshi.* 2 March 2019. www.shethepeople.tv/news/reshma-story-alone-acid-attack-survivor/. Accessed 14 Aug. 2021.

"Convention on the Elimination of All Forms of Discrimination against Women". *General Assembly Resolution 34/180.* 1979.

Hindustan Times Correspondent. *6 years after SC ban, acid still being sold openly.* 10 Jan.

2020. www.hindustantimes.com/cities/6-years-after-sc-ban-acid-still-being-sold-openly/story-ccCiqPbMbL5a4iDhYVtYAN.html. Accessed 2 Aug. 2021.

Kalantry, Sital and Kestenbaum, Jocelyn Getgen, "Combating Acid Violence in Bangladesh, India, and Cambodia." *Avon Global Center for Women and Justice and Dorothea S. Clarke Program in Feminist Jurisprudence. Paper 1.* 2011 http://scholarship.law.corncll.cdu/avon_clarke/1

Krishnan, Murali. "No sign of decline in the number of acid attacks against women in India" 2020. Accessed 2 Aug. 2021. www.rfi.fr/en/podcasts/international-report/20201023-l

Nguyen, K. "India's acid attack victims face long wait for justice." Thomson Reuters Foundation. 16 Sep. 2015. in.reuters.com/article/india-acid-attack-victims/indiasacid-attack-victims-face-long-wait-for-justice-idINKCN0RG1FO20150916. Accessed 14 Aug. 2021.

Qureshi, Reshma. *Being Reshma: The Extraordinary Story of an Acid-Attack Survivor Who Took the World by Storm.* Pan Macmilllon, 2018.

Roy, Pulaha. "India Saw Almost 1,500 Acid Attacks in Five Years." *India Today* 12 Jan. 2020. indiatoday.in. Accessed 7 June 2021.

Winter, George. *Corrosive Acid Attacks.* PDF. pp. 73-75. Accessed 23 Sep. 2021.

Wolf, Naomi. "The Beauty Myth. Vintage Books, 2013." *Google books.* Accessed 14 Aug. 2021.

World Health Organisation. "Violence against women" 9 March 2021.

www.who.int/news-room/fact-sheets/detail/violence-against-women. Accessed 14 Aug. 2021.

Zalmai, Ahmad Shakib, and Amiri Amiri. *Acid Attack and its Clinical and Psychological Effect. International Journal of Academic Research in Progressive Education and Development*, vol. 10, no. 3, pp. 11–19. 2021.

CHAPTER 5

Traversing through the Psyche: Reading of *Never Have I Ever* as a Trauma Narrative

Ms. Anju. M.B

The concept of trauma has its origin in the discipline of psychology in the early 1980s, especially in the works of Jean Martin Charcot, Sigmund Freud and Joseph Breuer. After the Vietnam War, psychologists began to analyse the connection between mental illness and trauma. The concept of trauma got popularity as it began to analyse the effects of trauma in the collective population after Holocaust and such horrifying historical events. It resulted in the emergence of the concept of Post Trauma Stress Disorder (PTSD). Around the 1990s, the concept of trauma became interdisciplinary, merging literature, history, sociology, etc. Cathy Caruth, Judith Herman, and Shoshanna Felaman developed the theoretical aspects of trauma narrative. Trauma studies secure a significant position in the current space of literature and theory. Literature gives vent to the untold trauma experiences in surprising ways. Recent developments in cinema and other visual mediums like television series and web series also focus on the representation of trauma. But, rarely do we come across an authentic and sensitive representation of trauma in popular culture. Movies like *First Blood* (1982), *Batman Begins* (2005) and series like *Ann With an* E (2017), *Sex Education* (2019) are known for the representation of trauma-driven characters. The seemingly light-hearted teenage romantic series *Never Have I Ever* (2020) exemplifies the complicated theme of trauma subtly.

The plot of *Never Have I Ever* falls into the genre of a comedy drama. Mindy Kaling and Lang Fisher are the creators of this television series. This American series is about the life of a teenage American girl of Indian descent, Devi Viswakumar, played by

Maitreyi Ramakrishnan. The series has two seasons, each with ten episodes. The series has been renewed for a third season. *Never Have I Ever* has an intriguing narrative style with the voice-over narration by John McEnroe, a legendary American tennis player. Reminding us of the chorus in the traditional Greek theatre, the omniscient narrator describes the events as well as comments on the actions of the characters. Devi's parents Nalini and Mohan played by Pooja Jagannathan and Sendhil Ramamurthy respectively, migrated to the United States from India in September 2001. "Her (Devi's) story starts when her parents, Nalini and Mohan moved to the United States in September 2001. Not a super-chill time to be a brown person in America" ("Pilot" 01:45). Here the narrative refers to the collective trauma associated with the 9/11 attack in the United States of America. Devi was born in America and she never thought of India as her homeland like her parents. Like any other first-generation Indian American, Devi experienced the dilemma of identity. Some people thought Devi was too Indian while others thought she wasn't Indian at all. "Even though Devi was Indian, she didn't think of herself as Indian...sometimes she felt out of place" ("Never Have I Ever Felt Super Indian" 06:40).

"Fundamentally, trauma is a wound" (Kurtz1). The traumatic event that wounded Devi's psyche was her father's unexpected death due to cardiac arrest. Devi worshipped her father. She was emotionally close to her father than her mother. Devi's father Mohan died right in front of her eyes, while she was performing on stage for her Spring Orchestra Contest at School. Devi, even though shattered by the incident, refuses to acknowledge the pain associated with it. Devi dismisses talking about the traumatic occurrence. Devi's therapist Dr. Jamie Ryan says to Devi,

> Devi, the reason I was enlisted by your doctors and your mother is to delve into some of the major events that have happened in your life over this last year. Now we have been seeing each other for months, and you still don't want to talk about your father ("Never Have I Ever Had Sex With Paxton Hall-Yoshida"02:06).

A week after Mohan's death Devi gets paralysed for no medical reason. "We think of trauma as a pathological and emotional condition, an injury to the psyche caused by catastrophic events or by the threat of such events, which overwhelm an individual's normal response mechanisms" (Kurtz 2). As Devi was paralysed for no medical reason, people thought that she was faking it. Her classmate and competitor at school Ben Gross comments "Do you know when you can't use your legs for no medical reason, it's called psychosomatic? which, my Dad says means fake". ("Pilot" 9:26) It is her repressed pain associated with her father's death that resulted in the psychosomatic symptom. Devi was paralysed for three months. Later the symptom disappears and Devi can walk again. But her psyche invents an escape mechanism from the trauma, which is Paxton Hall-Yoshida, played by Darren Barnet. Paxton is a high school heartthrob and Devi's classmate. Devi plans to have sex with him. At a superficial level, Devi's actions might seem like that of a spoiled teenager trying to be a rebel. But in reality it was the result of the devastating effect of the trauma on her psyche.

> A psychic trauma is caused when an intense, often extremely violent situation disables the ability of a consciousness to integrate an experience within the narrative, linear memory of an individual. The psyche is overwhelmed by negative impulses and stimuli to a degree that it cannot react adequately (Kohne 4).

The trauma of Mohan's death harms Devi's psyche so intensely that she no longer remains the person she used to be. She becomes emotionally reactive and exhibits temperament issues to the extent that people start calling her as Crazy Devi. Dr. Jamie Ryan suggests that Devi should keep a grief journal as Devi was not ready to talk about the pain that she experienced. "Sometimes the pain we feel is so hard to say out loud" ("Never Have I Ever"13:07). Doctor was hoping that Devi will vent out her suppressed emotions in the grief journal. Instead Devi writes about her plan to have sex with Paxton Hall-Yoshida in it. Devi exhibits post trauma stress disorder symptoms. Silvia Pellicer-Ortin in her essay titled 'The Ethical Clock of Trauma in Eva Figes' *Winter Journey* points out about PTSD; "The syndrome, which emerged from the treatment of Vietnam veterans was characterised in terms of 'intrusive symptoms' (such as nightmares, flashbacks and persistent memories), avoidance symptoms (such as emotional numbing, withdrawal from the world and avoidance of reminders) and symptoms of overarousal (such as insomnia and irritability)" (48). Devi exhibits these symptoms. She gets nightmares. She dreams about Mohan. Those two dream sequences are significant to the narrative as they give us an idea about the depth of bonding between Devi and her father. In the first episode of season one, a dream sequence is featured where Devi sees her father Mohan sitting on the sofa of the living room watching a match of John McEnroe, Mohan's favourite sportsperson. Devi asks Mohan "Dad, am I ugly?" to which Mohan replies "What nonsense. I'm looking at you right now. You're the most beautiful girl in the world" (16:53) Mohan consoles Devi and reassures her that she is good enough to fight with her spirit. At the end of the dream, Devi asks Mohan "What are you doing here?...you died" (16:58). Mohan replies "Oh, that. I'm better now. (16:59). Towards the end of the series, we witness Devi processing her trauma. In the final episode of Season two, Devi dreams about Mohan again. Devi was in trouble as she was not able to come to terms with her strange relationship with Paxton. He was ashamed of publicly accepting Devi as his girlfriend. She dreams about Mohan helping her to find a solution to the dilemma. Mohan says "I feel you could use some fatherly wisdom. I can tell your heart is a little heavy" ("Never Have I Ever Been a Perfect Girl" 14:00). Mohan advises Devi that her secret relationship with Paxton is not good for her. "The Devi I know would never agree to be someone's secret girlfriend kept in the shadows" (14:03). Devi's consciousness is unable to comprehend the trauma of her father's death. But deep down she is grieving and that pain is repressed in her psyche.

Historian Dominick LaCapra mentions the process of 'acting out' and 'working through' as the two main stages in the process of overcoming trauma (Santiago 88). The first season of the series presents the acting out stage, where she is forced to relive the traumatic event in an unconscious way. She gets nightmares, she is triggered by the sound of an ambulance, and certain slight references of the tragedy can disturb her. The second season can be seen as projecting Devi's 'working through' phase. Towards the end of season two, Devi is attempting to process the trauma, which she was dissociating with in the initial part of the narrative. Devi unconsciously uses Paxton as an escape mechanism, for not thinking about her father. She keeps on shutting down memories of Mohan. But she gets annoying flashbacks that disturb her mental balance. Devi is not able to enjoy a romantic moment with Paxton. Paxton kisses Devi on their way back to Devi's home from a night party. Devi was feeling ecstatic and joyous. As Devi enters the living room which was dark, she mistakes her uncle Aravind for her father. The narrative voice of John McEnroe says "Devi mistaking her uncle for her Dad had dung up a memory she'd buried deep inside. She was so rattled by it, she almost forgot a much more exciting new memory. She just kissed Paxton fricking Hall fricking Yoshida" ("Never Have I Ever Had to be on My Best Behavior" 02:22). A montage, which contains Mohan's disturbing face in the frame, the red headlight of an ambulance, Mohan's body on the stretcher is shown to represent Devi getting triggered by the flashbacks. She auto-suggests her mind to think about Paxton and about the kiss they just had. But that never happens, her Dad's memory takes control of her mind and Devi is unable to sleep. The next day her mother Nalini's dialogue with her triggers the memory back again. Nalini says "Devi, for once can you please try not to make my life any harder?" ("Never Have I Ever Had to be on My Best Behavior" 04:17) Nalini was referring to the incident where Devi mistook her uncle for Mohan and screamed at him. But that digs up a traumatic memory that occurred on the day when Mohan died. Devi and Nalini had a serious fight as Devi misplaced the music sheet that she needed for her concert performance. Devi shouts at her mother as she was told that she was grounded for two weeks for losing her music sheet. Mohan gets disturbed by the yelling and shouting by Devi and Nalini. Mohan asks both of them to calm down. Mohan says "...when we come home later, I will fix this" ("Never Have I Ever Had to be on My Best Behavior"10:04). But that fixing up never happens. Mohan dies at the concert due to cardiac arrest. "Devi had hoped she'd slept that memory off, but there it was again. Of all days, today she needed to be normal. So she had no choice but to shove that memory back down to where it came from" ("Never Have I Ever Had to be on My Best Behavior"04:53).Devi's mother Nalini considers getting emotionally vulnerable in front of your child as a sign of weakness. She is a controlling and dominating parent. Devi's trauma is transformed into anger towards her mother. Devi fights with her mother for her controlling nature. Devi says "I lost the only parent that actually cared about me. I wish you were the one that died that night" (22:52). Mohan's death was traumatic to Nalini also. But unlike Devi, Nalini never tried to escape from the pain. She undergoes the process of healing and it is presented as a very private affair. Yet there is a scene where Nalini's interaction with Devi's therapist plays a significant role in liberating her emotionally in its fullest sense.

Devi was unable to play the harp after the traumatic incident. Not just because Mohan died right in front of her while she was playing the harp at the music concert. It was Mohan who gifted her the harp when she was a small girl. "See this is an instrument for a real musician. You're far too special for a stupid guitar. Prodigy" ("Never Have I Ever Had to be on My Best Behavior"15:48). Devi's cousin Kamala's prospective groom visits their home. Devi's uncle Aravind asks Devi to play the harp. Nalini says Devi is taking a break from the harp hinting at the tragedy of Mohan's death. But somehow Devi had to play the harp to hide some mishap between Kamala and her boyfriend. As Devi tries tuning the harp, the montage of the traumatic event passes through her psyche. She struggles a lot, with memories of Mohan flashing through her mind. But somehow she manages to play the harp. The narrative voice says "Hey, this is kind of a breakthrough. Devi is playing the harp again? Maybe she's all better now" ("Never Have I Ever Had to be on My Best Behavior" 16:05).

Even though the series focuses on the individual trauma of Devi, there are references of collective trauma with occasional reference to certain historical events along with the main narrative. The main narrative of the series has history lectures as its background. Devi is a student of Sophomore. The geographical aspects of the narrative are basically confined to Devi's home and school in Southern California. A major part of representation of school in the narrative is shown as Devi and her classmates are attending history lectures of Mr. Shapiro. On the blackboard, it is written with chalk "Facing History and Ourselves" ("Pilot"10:16). Mr. Shapiro says "This is not gonna be your typical history class. We are going to be unpacking some very difficult subjects like slavery (points to Fabiola who is an African American) and the Holocaust (points to Ben Gross, who is a Jew). Think of this as a ride on a tour bus through some of the darkest moments of our history" (Pilot, 10:20). He also adds "As we travel through all of humanity's most horrific atrocities, I want you to feel shooketh" ("Pilot"10:47).

"The psycho-analytic understanding of trauma defines it as an event so overwhelming that it cannot be processed normally at the time of its occurrence so that its memory is effectively blocked but returns to haunt the victim until it is appropriately confronted and dealt with" (Kurtz, 3). There is a constant disagreement that Devi's psyche undergoes as the narrative proceeds. On one hand she dissociates with the trauma of Mohan's death, but on the other hand, she clings to the things that are closely linked to Mohan. The harp that he gifted Devi when she was a young girl, his vegetable garden,

Moped Scotter and his voice message on her mobile phone are some of them. A bunch of non-living things that are emotionally lively enough to trigger Devi with pesky flashbacks, but still she refuses to get rid of them. Devi happens to see a coyote at her father's vegetable garden and she believes that it is the reincarnation of her dead father. Later at her friend Trent's house, she sees a coyote and thinks that it is her father and approaches it. But the coyote attacks Devi.

The narrative of the series exclusively presents how trauma disrupts the identity of the character as well as his/her relationship with others. The narrative includes the personal history of Devi as well as her cultural history as a first-generation Indian-American. Devi's perspective towards social morals changes after the trauma. Dr. Jamie Ryan suggests that Devi is in need of inner peace and moral clarity ("Never Have I Ever Begged For Forgiveness" 04:01). Devi becomes emotionally insensitive to her best friends Fabiola and Eleanor, who stood with her through thick and thin. Devi's consciousness is unable to make proper decisions and her relationship dynamics with her best friends gets messed up. She lies to them and even treats them disrespectfully. Fabiola tells Devi; "You've turned into this fake person, who only cares about popularity and Paxton" ("Never Have I Ever Pissed off Everyone I Knew" 21:15). Eleanor says to Devi "We just miss our old friend but right now, you're not her. You just seem lost" ("Never Have I Ever Pissed off Everyone I Knew"21:47).

Dr. Jamie Ryan's therapy sessions with Devi is enlightening and sensitive.

> "Dr. Ryan: Devi, listen you were so traumatised by your dad's death, you lost the use of your legs for three months.
>
> Devi: Yeah I know. What does that have to do with anything?
>
> Dr. Ryan: This thing with your friends, baby girl, that's your grief.
>
> Devi: So, my dad dies, and suddenly my friends are bitches?
>
> Dr. Ryan: Devi, you are so desperate to not feel sad, you've made your whole world about this boy (Paxton).
>
> Devi: I am a teenager. My whole world is about boys.
>
> Dr. Ryan: I want you to allow yourself to acknowledge the pain you so clearly feel.

> Devi: So you're saying that I should get over my sadness by getting really sad? Why would I do that? So I can be miserable and realise the person I love the most is never ever coming back?
>
> Dr. Ryan: Yes, Because that would help you to heal" (Never Have I Ever Pissed off Everyone I Knew, (10:37-10:50).

"... it is a widely accepted therapeutic truth that the stories we tell about catastrophes that beset us both individual and collective can be crucial tool for recovery" (Pederson 97). A subplot in the series features Paxton's grandfather Theodore Yoshida's trauma and how he comes to terms with it. Paxton is half American and half Japanese. Paxton volunteers to do an assignment at school. The assignment was an oral presentation about one event in the great American saga that has personally affected the students and their family. Mr. Shapiro asks the students "Who is brave enough to face their history?" ("Never Have I Ever Stalked My Mother" 03:39). Paxton finds a diary that his grandfather Theodore Yoshida gave him that he never bothered to read before. Paxton calls his grandfather Ojichan. The diary contained memories of Ojichan's father, Paxton's great grandfather. He was forced to live in an internment camp with his family in Manzanar in 1944. Ojichan was a young boy when he was in an internment camp. He had a journal kept with him all the years written by his father. Paxton was emotionally moved as he read about the trauma that his great grandfather and grandfather had experienced. Paxton's grandfather never liked talking about his days in the camp, whenever someone asked about it he would shut them down. But after so many years of experiencing the trauma, finally, he speaks about it to his grandson's classmates and teacher. Paxton begins the narrative of trauma joined by his grandfather. "During World War II, right here in California, the government forced over 120,000 Japanese Americans to live in internment camps, My grandfather was one of them". ("Never Have I Ever Stalked My Mother" 14:48). Parallel to Devi and Mohan's bonding there is Theodore's relationship with his father and the trauma that he experienced. Theodore says that to see his father hurt was the most difficult part to be in the internment camp. He never talked about the trauma until now. "...I am one of the last people to still remember Manzanar, I need to tell my story so no one ever forgets" ("Never Have I Ever Stalked My Own Mother" 16:23).

Visual representation of trauma in popular culture is an area that is yet to be explored. The close-up shots, editing, montage everything brings together to represent the unpresentable psychological wound. Devi as a trauma victim finds it difficult to communicate. Finally, she acknowledges the pain and is willing to talk to Dr. Ryan. "The trauma thus requires integration, both for the sake of testimony and for the sake of cure" (Caruth 3). The narrative of the series skilfully blends in the traumatic experiences of Devi and Theodore, how both struggle hard to process the trauma and verbalise it.

Work Cited

Caruth, Kathy. "Introduction". *Trauma -Explorations in Memory.* edited by Caruth, Kathy. The John Hopkins University Press, 1995, https://hemi.nyu.edu/hemi/ images/courses/spring-2009/caruthintro.pdf

Kurtz, J.Roger. "Introduction" *Trauma and Literature.* edited by Kurtz, J Roger. Cambridge University Press, 2018, *https://literariness.org/wp-content/uploads/2021/04/Literariness.org-Trauma-and-Literature-Edited-by-J.-Roger-Kurtz-CUP-2018-1.pdf*

Never Have I Ever. Created by Mindy Kaling and Lang Fisher, performance by Maitreyi Ramakrishnan, Kaling International. Inc. Netflix, 2020.

Ortin, Silvia Pellicer. "The Ethical Clock of Trauma in Eva Figes' *Winter Journey*". *Trauma in Contemporary British Fiction, edited* by Onega, Susana and Jean Michael. Brill, 2011, Google Books, https://www.google.co.in/books/ edition/_/ MamkWXm8IWIC?hl=en&gbpv=1&pg=PA1&dq=individual+ trauma+analysis+in+fiction

Pederson, Joshua. "Trauma and Narrative" *Trauma and Literature.* edited by Kurtz, J Roger. Cambridge University Press, 2018, *https://literariness.org/wp-content/uploads/2021/04/Literariness.org-Trauma-and-Literature-Edited-by-J.-Roger-Kurtz-CUP-2018-1.pdf*

Santiago, Miriam Fernandez. "'Acting Out' and 'Working Through' Departure in Thomas Pynchon's Bleeding Edge". *Nordic Journal of English Studies* 2019, 18(2):86-110,file:///C:/Users/Isha/AppData/Local/Temp/516-596-1-SM.pdf

CHAPTER 6

Traumatising Love: An Exploration of K. R. Meera's *The Poison of Love*

Athira. S. S

Trauma is a kind of psychological injury that affects a person's capacity to feel and also his sense of self. Traumatic experiences are usually an extremely painful event that is capable enough to shatter the person emotionally and physically. As Greening quotes, "when we experience trauma, our relationship with existence itself is shattered (324)". Recently the term trauma has become a key term in psychoanalytic approaches to literary study. Trauma theory gained attention as an interdisciplinary field of study in the mid 1990s with the publication of works by Cathy Caruth and Kali Tal. The concept of trauma transcended the boundaries and achieved relevance in the field of literature when the writers made a literal representation of the traumatic disturbances of the characters in their works.

Love is the most wonderful among the feelings which one can experience. The real love will make a person more secure as it is built on mutual respect and companionship. The success of true love depends upon two people who really understand and care for each other to have a healthy love relationship. Each person may experience love in different ways. But at times, love can be painful and traumatic. The emotional scars left behind by the love relationship can pave way for extreme traumatic disturbances in individual psyche and consequently it will affect the person's quality of life. In this type of traumatic suffering, memories from the past intrudes too much on the present life and will influence the person's thoughts, feelings and behaviour. Love, the most powerful source of pleasure can also be a source of extreme pain and grief in the life of certain people.

The novel *The Poison of Love* is an engrossing tale of love and betrayal and it follows the journey of Tulsi from a self-assured individual to a totally devastated woman who was fully blinded by the love of her charming and eloquent husband. The novel was written by K. R. Meera in Malayalam as *Meerasadhu* and it was translated into English by Ministhy. S. Meera is a significant writer in Malayalam who uses her writings as a medium to portray the struggles faced by women in the contemporary Indian society. Her writings advocate the need of women empowerment since her writings portray female characters who were strong enough to break free from the shackles of traditional patriarchal society. In *The Poison of Love* also she was able to create a powerful woman who was able to break away from the strong clutches of love that tried to strangle her all through her life.

Tulsi, the protagonist of the novel meets Madhav for the first time when she was seventeen years old and at that time she was an IIT student and Madhav was a correspondent with an English magazine in Chennai. They develop a friendship after their first meeting and Tulsi was too much amused when Madhav openly confesses about his twenty seven lovers who came after him pleading for his love. It is only after her marriage was fixed with Vinay that Madhav expresses his love for Tulsi claiming that she is the one whom he was searching all through his life. He entices Tulsi with his charming words and it urged Tulsi to elope with him just days before her marriage with Vinay. The relationship which was a very happy and passionate one at the beginning turned out to be a disastrous and traumatic one for Tulsi when the real character of Madhav is revealed before her. Madhav was such a cunning man as he deceived Tulsi with his words of love while continuing his romantic relationships with other women. With his charming appearance and enticing words he made Tulsi completely dependent upon himself and his love. Tulsi who had sacrificed everything for Madhav was totally devastated by this betrayal and this shock paved way for certain traumatic disturbances that affected her physically and mentally.

Madhav is the kind of man who uses the tactic of love-bombing to win the heart of women he desires. Love-bombing is the technique of giving excessive admiration, affection and attention to the partner so as to make them feel more dependent on that person. It is the practice of overwhelming the other with extreme affection and admiration. The person may shower the other with attention, love, gifts and all sorts of romantic things as to show the intensity of their love. But as the days pass this intensity will evaporate leading the other to undergo a series of traumatic struggles. Madhav uses this manipulative technique throughout his relationship with Tulsi. When Tulsi's marriage with Vinay is fixed, Madhav expresses his love for her and was able to dissuade her from the marriage with his enticing words. He claims that no one could ever love Tulsi as he does and promises a happy life after marriage. His manipulative attitude is very evident in his reply to Tulsi's statement as whenever she thinks of Madhav what she could imagine is a room full of women behind him. He replies:

> Tulsi, I shall never refuse any woman's love. It would devastate her. If my love can make a woman happy, why would I want to deny her? You do not understand, Tulsi. They were all unhappy. They had never been loved. They had been denied love by their fathers, husbands or sweethearts. I offered them my love as alms. This body of mine will be eaten by ants and worms one day. If it can be of use to another human being, why should I refuse? But be clear about this------I never desired any of them. I never demanded anything from them either (17).

Tulsi was enchanted by the words of Madhav like a Gopika who was enchanted by the divine music of Krishna's flute. It is as if she was under some sort of black magic. Even after their marriage, he continued showering his affection upon Tulsi. His love was like acid that corroded her body completely and by burning her flesh it dissolved her completely into him. But it was too late when Tulsi realised Madhav's original character as a man of cunningness and manipulation. Tulsi who loved Madhav with all her heart was unable to bear this betrayal and her happy days with him began to haunt her continuously leaving her mentally upset.

Within three years of their marriage Tulsi realised that her conviction of being Madhav's final lover was just an illusion but by then she had lost everything, her family as well as her career. She got the first indication of her losses when she was pregnant with her first child Unni. While she was in the bedroom she noticed a steady procession of corpse-eating ants entering the wardrobe where Madhav stores his documents. The ants were behind a black snake with a half swallowed rat in its mouth. This scene of the ants eating both the predator and the prey had a disturbing impact on her mind. This incident was symbolic of the futuristic traumatic disturbances which she had to encounter as a result of her all-consuming love for Madhav. The documents in the wardrobe were actually the love letters written by Madhav's countless girlfriends. When Tulsi questioned Madhav about this he was able to convince her through his enticing words and her suspicions were melted away like butter. Whenever she broaches the topic, he would say, "I am yours...I belong to you physically, emotionally, legally...my child is growing in your womb. Why these frivolous doubts then?"(63). At first Tulsi was convinced by his sweet words. But gradually she lost faith in him and it began to disturb her mentally leaving her worried and upset all the time.

Love is the kind of emotion which has the power to strengthen as well as to weaken an individual. In the case of Tulsi, love makes her more weak and helpless. She became more silenced and dreams began to haunt her. Nightmares are a major aspect of traumatic disturbances as people who are affected by trauma are often disturbed by dreams and nightmares as a reflection of their fear and anxiety. Tulsi says, "I would wake up, drenched in sweat, from a recurring nightmare; women with heavy bottoms---like corpse-eating ants that walked on two legs--- were all over Madhav (63)". When she realised Madhav's relation with other women, she was tense with the fear of losing her husband. She was full of love for him that she could not even think about losing him. Gradually a glass barrier developed between them and he became more distant and their conversations became a mere ritual. Her past life continued to haunt her through her dreams. Just before going to Mathura, while she was in hotel, she dreams of her ancestral home in a loathsome way. The dream was about a Salem mango tree in her home and it is described as,

> The sight of the splendid mango blossoms filled me with joy. Suddenly causing the earth to quake, a monstrous black snake slithered down from amidst the mango blooms. Partly uncoiling itself, it began to swing menacingly from a low branch. The tip of its black tail reached my feet. It raised the three-hooded head that was huge as an elephant's and reared it as high as the house itself. The middle hood was white. The three forked tongues flicked out blood red, splayed fearsomely against the sky. (33)

Dreams are a major aspect of traumatic struggles as dreams serves as a medium for the individual to get a reflection of his anxiety and fear. The shock that Tulsi received through her passionate love for Madhav finds its expression in the series of dreams that Tulsi sees. She also dreams of those days when Madhav used to shower her with extreme love and affection. Her past life with Madhav intrudes into her present through the dreams which she encounters.

The glass barrier formed between Tulsi and Madhav turned into a granite one when she was pregnant with her second child. Madhav stopped coming home and there were numerous stories spreading about him associated with many women. But by then her mind was full of intense pain and she was at the brink of losing her mind. All these days Tulsi was extremely depressed and worried as she cannot let go of her love for Madhav. She returns to her paternal home with her second child as she was fed up with this pain of love. But then also Madhav was able to convince her through his manipulative words to accompany him to their home. "Madhav's calls began after that. 'Where have you kept my razor, Tulsi? My towel? My shirts? Trousers? Coats? Which coat should I wear with the ash-coloured shirt, Tulsi? You have misunderstood me. The truth is very different. Your suspicions debilitate me. Just be sure of one thing. I have no life without you or my children. You are my strength (84)". It was a weakness from Tulsi's part that she devoted herself wholly to Madhav without realising his cunningness. It was too late when she recognised that for the real Madhav, Tulsi was just an ordinary woman among his other lovers who were popular and rich.

It is at the request of a television anchor who was pregnant with Madhav's child that Tulsi decides to separate from him. By that time Tulsi was totally devastated and her love turned out to be the chief cause for her painful condition. Tulsi was a woman who sacrificed everything for love. Her life was completely dependent upon Madhav and his love so much so that when Madhav put forward the thought of divorce, she felt as if her very existence is shattered. She imagined herself returning to her father's home as an exhausted body with sunken eyes. After Madhav left the house with his belongings, she tried her best to forget him but the wounds failed to heal. It is during this situation that her traumatising struggles reached its zenith. It is at the most extreme moment of her pain that she kills her children by adding poison in the milk. She lost control of her state of mind and it is evident through her reaction when Madhav realises the death of children:

> He screamed in horror. I was stark naked. With my long hair flying free, I laughed uproariously. I went round and round the room. The earth went round and round with me. Our king-sized bed turned round and round. The fan, the sofa and the wardrobe that held the love letters from Madhav's girlfriends---all went round and round. The deadbodies of my children, crawling all over with ants, went round and round. Everything went round and round. (94-95)

The pain of love that caught hold of Tulsi was so intense that it forced her to kill her own children and end up in the Psychiatric ward of Trivandrum Medical College. It is at this severe state of traumatic condition that Tulsi boards bus to Mathura and reaches Vrindavan.

The women living in Vrindavan are the best instances of traumatic aspects of love. They are old women or widows who found solace at the feet of Lord Krishna. The woman named Nabaneeta whom Tulsi meets in Vrindavan is also a victim of love-trauma as she was abandoned by her lover at Kashi. She was abused by many men until she reached Vrindavan. Likewise all the women in Vrindavan have their own share of pain and most of them are wounded by love. Even after being hurt by love, many of them found solace in the love of Lord Krishna but Nabaneetha warns all other 'meerasadhus' that even Krishna is a cheat since all the women are same for him and he will pretend to love all of them. It is her wounded mind that made her to think indifferently about love.

After reaching Vrindavan also Tulsi was deeply disturbed by her past life and she found out some sort of escape from this pain by physically hurting herself. While in the temple she used to fight with monkeys for fruits thrown by the visitors and it results in some grievous wounds. She says, "The wounds I sustained during these scuffles became badly infected and hurt grievously. The pain delighted me (5)." It is through this physical agony that she got some kind of relief from her mental troubles.

The intense traumatic pain of Tulsi found a way out through her vengeance to Madhav. It is this pain that made Tulsi wait for twelve years in Vrindavan for Madhav. She had spent every single day recalling her memories and thinking of each and every moment of her life with Madhav. She says: "My body was dead. The single throb of life in it was my malicious hatred for him. One day my retribution would be complete. He would come to me with filth all over his body. I would dip him in the dark Yamuna of my vengeance. I would wash away the memories of my children (69)." She considered Madhav as her enemy and believed that it is only through her present devastated condition that she could hurt Madhav. When she finally met Madhav at Vrindavan he was completely shocked to see her "missing front teeth, sunken eyes, skinny bag of body, tonsured head and torn sari (6)". In order to complete her revenge she crawled on all fours towards him and begged for alms. This shocked Madhav and he was admitted in the hospital due to heart attack. Tulsi who once loved

Madhav with all her heart has become completely unsympathetic in her feeling for Madhav that she refused to meet him when he was in the hospital. It is only to fulfil her revenge that she meets him at the hospital in the end. Even then she was unaffected by his manipulative words and she bursts out laughing when he asked her to return to his life. This uncontrollable laughter is an outcome of the extreme pain which she encountered due to his love.

Tulsi who was a successful IIT Graduate has become a helpless 'meerasadhu' in Vrindavan only due to her love for Madhav. The emotion of love which has the power to strengthen a human being has a very disastrous effect in the life of Tulsi. Love serves as the root cause for all her agonies. It is her endless love for Madhav that made her lose her family, her children, her career, and even her self-respect. She had to undergo certain traumatic disturbances as part of her relationship with Madhav. One of the most important things regarding Tulsi is that she was able to find a way out from her emotional struggles by escaping from the clutches of Madhav. It is evident from Tulsi's words that she could never forget Madhav and his love, even then she was able to take revenge upon him by ignoring him completely and leading life as a 'meerasadhu'. She was able to break free the strangling clutches of Madhav inspite of all his manipulative words of love. She stands out as a strong woman who was able to regain her selfhood after a long term of struggles which was part of her love relationship. This paper explores how love served as a major factor in creating traumatic disturbances in Tulsi's life and it also focuses on her struggles to escape from the strong clutches of love that tried to strangle her.

Work Cited

Bajwa, Rupa. "The Well of Loneliness." *The Hindu.* 15 April 2017.

https://www.thehindu.com/books/books-reviews/the-well-of-loneliness/article18058199.ece

Caruth, Cathy. *Unclaimed Experiences: Trauma, Narrative and History.* Johns Hopkins University Press, 1996.

Greening, Thomas. "PTSD from the perspective of existential –humanistic psychology." *Journal of Traumatic Stress.* Vol. 3, no. 2, April 1990. Pp. 323-326.

Meera, K. R. *The Poison of Love.* Translated by Ministhy. S, Penguin Books, 2017.

CHAPTER 7

Memory, Body and Women: Trauma in Nalini Malani's Art

V. Kezia Anna

Nalini Malani's works present a sustained cycle of violence, which is disturbing on one hand and is meditative on the other. There is an unending, and successive violence in human history that Malani's works engage with; where the absent-present, memory, tradition, body and women's experiences are represented. Her retelling and questioning of history give voice to the marginal. The artist herself has a complex inheritance, having the status of a refugee in a newly independent India. Her visual imagery is therefore often fraught with the trauma of partition. She juxtaposes her experiences, memories and ideologies across time and space, creating a globalised narrative, with a complex assimilation of the universal, as well as the subjective, in her visual narrative of pain, suffering, mutilation, dissections and disfigurations. Women and the feminine also figure prominently in her visuality. Rape, honour killing, migration, acid attack, and other brutalities figure in her representations, with body, in all its dimensions represented through her art including blood, gut and human entrail, reinforcing trauma. This article titled "Memory, Body and Women: Trauma in Nalini Malani's Art" reads into the aspects that make her works a dialogue on the experiences of trauma.

As an artist, Nalini Malani is as versatile as any artist can be, in her choice of mediums. Painting is her base. In an interview at the 51st Venice Biennale, she says;

> I paint therefore I am. … The language that probes other material is extended through painting. I work with de-forming the colors in video - keying them in as I would with watercolors. Or as my work in reverse painting – 'throwing' colors, embedding them into the supports. I am not interested in the mimetic, which is a given factor in this medium. For example, in "Hamletmachine" the colors 'bleed 'into each other over the body of the protagonist. In a number of my works there is as well an overlay of hand-drawn animation. The threshold between additive and subtractive light is blurred. (Pijnappel, Johan)

Conversely, in the artist's statement in the exhibition catalogue of *Text and Subtext,* she states:

> I do not think of myself as a painter. Drawing/painting works for me as a keyboard would for the music composer. It helps me to dream – to free associate – to flow into reveries; it helps me to compose ideas that can then work with creating all-encompassing environments. (Malani, Nalini)

This fluidity is precisely because of the diversity in the mediums she uses and experiments with. She has painted on canvas, walls, paper, glass and mylar. She has made large video installations with several reels of imagery simultaneously channeled onto screens and monitors. She has made accordion books using photocopy, monotype, painting and drawing. She has also made artist books. She has collaborated with actors, designers, directors, and musicians to create immersive environments through theatrical productions She has also made single-channel animated videos, drawing and erasing images several hundred times in the process. And she has created painted installations using revolving mylar cylinders.

Malani's art deals with the personal and the universal, local and the global as well as culturally specific and internationally known. Her videos and animations often use materials derived from various sources and from diverse times and places. Her works are a statement of her politics and ideas. The artist initiates the viewers into her world using immersive techniques, facilitating a dialogue through images, colours, and sounds. Her method of erasing and re-drawing images engages the viewer in the act of violence and remembering. The overlapping of different materials, videos, sounds and imageries also effects mnemonic associations in the viewer. It also reiterates artist's intensely political act.

In the essay, "Apocalypse Recalled: The Recent Work of Nalini Malani" Malani's art is succinctly described:

> As with all things that she engages with, Malani subjects this diverse body of poetry, ritual and art to alchemical processes, probing the veils of semblance and the limits of representation. The corpus of stories and images she deals with is put under intense pressure to the point of liquefaction, creating strange blends of science and fiction, history and myth, and generating a visual language that plumbs dystopia as an inevitable element of the present, and perhaps, as the ultimate fate of the world. There is no salvation at the end of the story; there is no eventual redemption in a triumph of good over evil. There is not even the conceit of the believing eye which is able to see good and evil as separate entities. (Sambrani, Chaitanya)

This unending, cyclic trauma is not intended to be cathartic, but meditative, like the Tibetan prayer wheels, which has been a leitmotif in many of her works. In the artist's own words in an interview with Ann McCoy for *The Brooklyn Rail*:

> I don't use the cathartic method. I actually use different shades of seduction to draw the person in…[T]here is a strange balance in my shadow plays between the contents of violence opposite the feeling of non-violence as one experiences in Tibetan praying wheels.

Memory and Re-telling of Stories in Nalini Malani's Art

Nalini Malani's works deals with the porous nature of memory, both the personal and the collective. Malani has always tried to engage with tradition to retell stories in her paintings, installations and other works, which engages with memory. She takes up epics, mythology, and religion, along with social incidents, newspaper stories, literature, films, and historical moments to retell a moment. This engages the viewers, who anticipates what will come next. Malani not only retell stories in a new form, but also in new configurations. Her artistic process is such that she wants to reclaim the right to represent history, tradition and memories in her own terms.

Memory ignites a potent historical discourse in Malani's works. There is often the burden of received/inherited memory that works with the everyday. The present, everyday and the familiar as well as the historical is critiqued. This is done by fusing together diverse memories and Malani is often seen to go against the grain. Her responses to the memories are not just personal but forms part of a larger whole. The idea of "postmemory" is important in this context.

Malani expresses her idea of memory in various works. A detail of *All We Imagine is Light* reads "Your memory comes in the way of my history". In the animation video *Memory: Record/ Erase* (1996), an interpretation of *The Job,* by Bertolt Brecht she records the fluid and porous nature of memories and thereby identities.

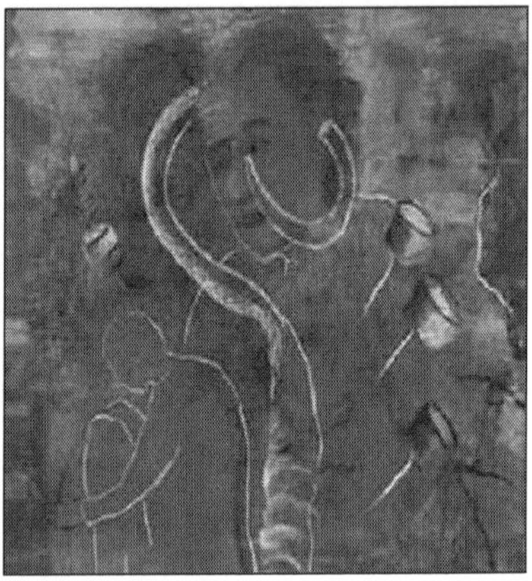

Fig 1: *All We Imagine as Light* (detail), (2017). © the artist.
Image Courtesy: Anil Rane
Fig 2, Fig 3: *Memory: Record/ Erase* (1996). © the artist.

Marianne Hirsch's "The Generation of Postmemory" talks about the """guardianship" of a traumatic personal and generational past with which some of us have a "living connection" and that past's passing into history" (2). She examines how trauma and memory are transferred intergenerationally. The generation which comes after, bears the personal, collective, and cultural trauma of those who came before. This would be through stories, images and behaviours among which they grew up. Individuals who feel a connection to traumatic historical occurrences that came before them actuate their remembrance of such histories through their present-day lived experience. This is precisely what Malani experiences and explicates in her works of art. In Art Review Asia featuring Nalini Malani, her words echo this postmemory:

> """History does not occur in episodes," Malani declares. When asked about her relationship to Partition, and the narrative of trauma and displacement that is often applied to her work, she continues, "I am more interested in how Partition activates itself in the present moment." When referring to the events of 15 August 1947, Malani says "Partition/Independence", as though the two words are interchangeable. She is often described as a Pakistani artist, but was born in Karachi in 1946 before the country was even formed. In 1947 her family was forced to leave for Calcutta (now Kolkata). "I have never had the desire to go back to the cities and villages my parents were from," she says. "But my mother, at ninety-six, still talks about it. It is not my trauma, but I have

grown up with the smell of those cities. Their aura.'"' (Thomas, Skye Arundhati)

Malani's *Remembering Toba Tek Singh* (1998) was a response to the Pokhran nuclear test carried out that same year and inspired by a short story by Sa 'adat Hassan Manto. Violence of the partition of India, archival materials based on Hiroshima and Nagasaki, montages from different countries featuring migration, rioting, suffering, crossing borders and loss are featured in her video installation. Tin trunks in grid formation also remind one of the traumas of the refugees. Memories of partition, war, nuclear technology fuses to bring out this trauma.

Fig 4: *Remembering Toba Tek Singh*,1998,
video installation. © the artist. Courtesy: Galerie Lelong & Co, New York & Paris

The conception and memory of nation state as a unified whole is also brought into question by Malani. As an artist, she prefers to remember the nation also as a flawed one, with all its failings and schisms that causes suffering and trauma. A romanticised notion of the nation is rejected in works like the video *Unity in Diversity* (2003). This video installation was a response to the Gujarat riots of March 2002. She brings in Ravi Varma's famed *Galaxy of Musicians* (1893), where an orchestral arrangement featuring Indian women from diverse cultural and ethnic backgrounds come together underscoring unity and nationalism. Malani uses this and reimposes the brutalities against the Muslim minorities in Gujarat in her video, highlighting the political horrors that the state and law unleashed.

Her personal memories/postmemories coalesce with the collective memory re-inventing history, nationalism, and tradition.

The multiplicity of experiences and reclaiming history are evident in her art. Christine Vial Kayser in "Nalini Malani, a Global Storyteller" quotes the artist:

> Emphasizing the link between the individual and the collective, Malani hereby manifests the importance of living communities, as well as of bodily sensations and emotions, in the construction of a particular memory. She says: Memory is what you are, past is in the present and in the future. Memory means the collective Memory – Memory of the race, Memory of the community"

Woman and Trauma in Nalini Malani's Art

Body and women are a predominant feature of Nalini Malani's art. Mythical images of Medea, Cassandra or Sita offers a complex view of the conflicts and violence within human psyche. Other than these mythical figures the experiences of women recur in her works. In her video installation *Unity in Diversity* (2003), the idyllic Ravi Varma scene disintegrates into violence and confusion of the partition and Gujarat communal violence. Visceral images of abortion distort Ravi Varma's women which is a reference to the rape, abduction, and mutilation of thousands of women. The violent reality of nationhood as experienced by Indian women is depicted here.

There is also the image of two women, one Indian and the other Pakistani, facing each other. They are engaged in a similar domestic task, that of folding a saree. This shared gesture reveals their kinship beyond all violence that man creates, also reinforcing the idea that women are left out of all decision-making processes, with women carrying the symbols of life and restraint. War and death are the prerogative of men and the women often bear the brunt of it. This display is also a tribute to the women stuck in war and exile, who still take care of the families.

Disfiguration of women's bodies, mutated beyond recognition, and often depicted beyond conventions of gender marks her female bodies as sites of pain. The *Mutant* series (1996), *Unity in Diversity* (1998) and *Mother India: Transactions in the Construction of Pain* (2005) all feature these aspects. *Mother India: Transactions in the Construction of Pain* (2005) is inspired by an essay by the sociologist Veena Das titled "Language and Body: Transactions in the Construction of Pain". Here too, partition and Gujarat riots are brought together. Images of the birth of the nation like Gandhi's spinning wheel, fades into scenes of destruction like the image of a gutted house. There is one scene where the image of a woman is juxtaposed against the map of

India and Pakistan, with the partition lines disfiguring her face. The violence is implicit here. The voice that reverberates also reiterates this violence. A female voice says that she died at the border of a new nation carrying a bloody rag as her flag.

Fig 5, Fig 6: *Mother India Transactions in the Construction of Pain*, 2005, video installation. © the artist.

Female trauma is again represented in *In Search of Vanished Blood* (2012) which is a large-scale installation featuring video images, floating shadows, and sound. The Greek character Cassandra is the narrator and there is a chaotic confluence of images. The shadow play using revolving Mylar cylinders also makes the viewers a part of the artistic process as bodies are bathed in colours and shadows. Women's voices from the past and present can be seen. In a piece, a poem is projected on a woman's face, which has been clothed like it is being hijacked and inflicted with pain. The reference of rape and other visceral imagery like autopsy tools conveying the idea of dissection, the organs which speaks of different emotions, invasive examinations that are an aftermath of rape – all speak of a cycle of violence and trauma that keep repeating across centuries.

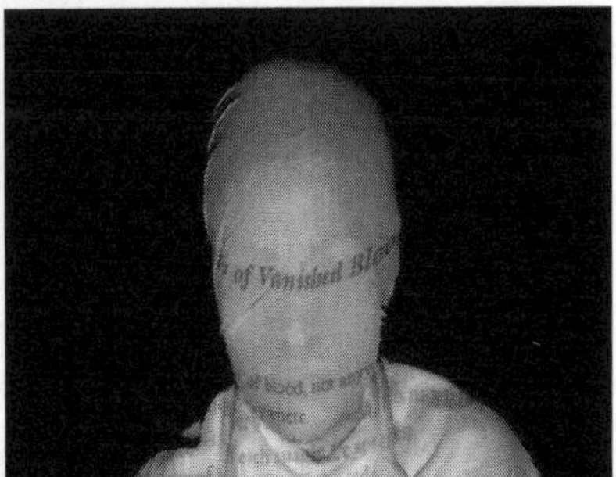

Fig 7, Fig 8: *In Search of Vanished Blood* (detail), 2012, installation, © the artist, Courtesy of Galerie Lelong, New York.

In her *Mutant* series of 1994-96, she explores women's bodies as sites of pain. The maternal body figures in this series as they produce mutant jelly – like offspring referencing the effect of the US nuclear testing in Marshall Islands, leading to malformations. Another video, *Stains* (2002) features the female figures painted on milk cartons, violent maternal bodies with guns in their hands, and stains depicting blood and fluids, projection on a massive latex breast, all explores the women's experience. The female body as a metaphor of violence is expressed in all these installations.

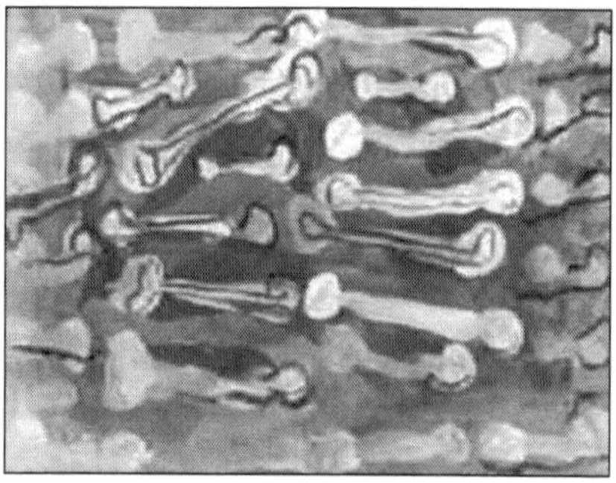

Fig 9, Fig 10, Fig 11: *Stains*, 2002, Animation Video Installation, © the artist.

Nalini Malani thus works with excesses. The human flaws in its perpetration of violence and the bloodbath in its process of creating boundaries, wars, nuclear weapons, and nationhood create sites of trauma and suffering. The women's bodies in this regard are specially depicted. The visceral and immersive quality of her work forces the viewer to take part in the unimaginable horrors of human life. Malani's works are a constant flow of dialogue between the poetic and the beautiful set against the brutality of existence.

Works Cited

Hirsch, Marianne. *The Generation of Postmemory*, Poetics Today2 9:1 (2008): 106. Retrieved https://read.dukeupress.edu/poetics-today/article/29/1/103/20954/ The-Generation-of-Postmemory

Kayser, Christine Vial. "Nalini Malani, a Global Storyteller". *Studies in Visual Arts and Communication: an international journal.* Vol 2, No 1 (2015) on-line. Retrieved www.journalonarts.org 1

Malani, Nalini, artist's statement, *Text and Subtext: International Contemporary Asian Women Artists Exhibition*, (Curator: Binghui Huangfu), exhibition catalogue, Singapore: Earl Lu Gallery, 2000, p. 62.

.... *Mother India: Transactions in the Construction of Pain.* Video Installation, 5 Projections, 5 1/2 mins, 2005.

.... *Remembering Toba Tek Singh.* Video Installation, 20 minutes looped, sound, 1998-99.

.... *Stains.* Animation Video Installation, 8½ minutes looped, sound, 2002.

.... *Unity in Diversity.* Video Installation, 7 ½ minutes looped, sound, 2003.

.... *Memory: Record/Erase.* Animation Video, 10 minutes, looped, sound, 1996.

McCoy, Ann. *Interview with Nalini Malani.* The Brooklyn Rail, November 2013 Issue. Retrieved

https://brooklynrail.org/2013/11/art/nalini-malani-with-ann-mccoy

Pijnappel, Johan, *Interview with Nalini Malani from the iCon India Catalogue produced for the Indian show at the 51 Venice Biennale.* Retrieved http://www.nalinimalani.com/texts/venice.htm

Sambrani, Chaitanya. *Apocalypse recalled: the recent work of Nalini Malani.* Retrieved http://www.nalinimalani.com/texts/chaitanya.htm

Thomas, Skye Arundhati. *Feature on Nalini Malani.* ArtReview Asia, 21 December 2017. Retrieved https://artreview.com/ara-winter-2017-feature-nalini-malani/

CHAPTER 8

The Psychological Conflict Underwent by the Mother in *Mother Of 1084*

K S Chitra

Mahasweta Devi was one of India's foremost literary figures from the late 20th and early 21st centuries. She was not only an eminent Bengali writer but was also a famous social activist. She was born on 14th January 1926 in Dhaka, Bangladesh. After her first schooling at Dhaka, Devi moved to West Bengal. In the year 1944 she got B A from Asutosh College. Devi attended Rabindranath Tagore-founded Viswa Bharati University and completed BA in English and then finished an MA in English at Calcutta University. Devi was deeply influenced by the communist movement of 1940's. She studied the life history of the rural tribal communities in India. Most of her research was widely based on the life of tribal communities of West Bengal. She extended her research and contributed a very good number of works which dealt with the oppression of women and dalits.

Devi's works focus on the struggles that determined women under the pretext of marginalisation and oppression. She herself being a woman is very well aware of the brutal treatments that woman undergoes both from the side of her family and the society which she lives in. Mahasweta Devi is a leading figure of the realm of art in the post-independent era. Mahasweta Devi becomes the voice of the unvoiced, shouting out the striking realities of their lives.

Mahasweta Devi wrote over 100 novels and over 20 collections of short stories, primarily written in Bengali but often translated into other languages. Her famous works include *Jhansi Rani, Hajar Churashir Maa, Satyadayini,* etc. She received the Jnanpith award, India's highest literary honour in the year 1966. She was also awarded the Ramon Magsaysay award in 1977 for her "compassionate crusade through art and activism to claim for tribal peoples, a just and honourable place in India's national life".

Studies prove that even though men are stronger than women in physical aspects, women are considered to be extremely stronger in the case of mental or emotional aspects. A woman could tolerate and withstand those emotional conflicts that she undergoes, under the pretext of society and even by her family members. A woman could bear any accusations that are made against her, but she will never tolerate something that matters to the members of her family. The female characters of Mahasweta Devi are never cowards. They are very brave and they try to tackle all their problems. Even though they feel themselves to be very low, in unbearable situations, they rise up and fight against those darkness in their way. Women are the only living creatures on earth who are praised and lowered equally. A woman is an epitome of all the best qualities. A girl attains fulfilment of her life when she becomes a mother. Life of a woman is very tragic, it is not that easy. Girls are taught even from their childhood days to tolerate and be patient to everything and everyone who torments them. A girl, who becomes a mother naturally by the qualities of a mother within her, starts living for her child.

The play *Mother of 1084* is a dramatisation of the novel entitled *Hajar Churashir Maa* written in Bengali. The plot of the story revolves around the character named Sujata, the mother mentioned in the title of the play who goes in search of the reason which led to the death of her son Brati Chatterjee, marked with the number 1084 by the police in the police morgue. The play tells the tragic story of Sujata Chatterjee, an upper class wife and mother who is informed of her youngest son Brati's death on his birthday. Her entire family including her husband Dibyanath, son and two daughters are never concerned about it and they try to suppress the nature of his death. All the family members except Sujata are afraid because Brati was killed in a police encounter along with the boys who are suspected to be naxalites. Sujata, who is informed about the death of her son, is asked to come to the police station to identify the dead body of her own son. She pleads with her family members to take her to the police station but none of them accompany her and moreover she is denied taking the car to the police station. At the police station she identifies her son as the corpse numbered 1084. Even after the body being recognised by Sujata, the police refuses to give the dead body of Brati to Sujata.

The remaining part of the play revolves around Sujata's question to find out how her son was killed and what was the reason that led to the murder of her son. This guides her and the readers to get into the origins of the movement and its ideology from a humanist perspective. On her way to her destiny, Sujata gets into contact with the mother of another boy who was also killed along with her son Brati. Sujata also gets to know about her son's girlfriend Nandhini. As the play proceeds, we find Sujata being alienated from her class conscious society and her family. This paper "The Psychological Conflict Underwent by the Mother in "Mother of 1084" " focuses on the trauma undergone by Sujata, in the due course of uncovering the truth behind her son's death. In the ending of the play Sujata dies.

The play is actually to be read in the context of Naxalite movement that happened in West Bengal in 1970's. The movement had its origin in the village of Naksalbari in 1967, when armed tribals began to revolt against the cruel practices of powerful landlords. The protests spread across Bengal with many students and young people joining the movement. The movement was ruthlessly suppressed by the state and brutal violence was unleashed. The protestors were arrested and put into jail and tortured severely. Many protestors were killed in fake encounter by the police as like Brati, in the play. The play is a recreation of the history of the marginalised and misrepresented Naxalite movement.

Sujata Chatterjee, is an upper class wife and mother of Brati. She comes from a family of conservative background. The life of Sujatha is actually a world filled with happiness not for her but in the eyes of the entire world. What actually Sujata feels about her life is that she is not living a life but a lie. She is not happy with the life that she leads with her womaniser husband and also with her children who behave indifferently to her except her youngest son Brati.

According to Sujata, in her own words

"I stand all alone in the family" (138).

This could be understood in the first scene when the police questions Sujata regarding her son Brati and ask her to go to Kantapukur to identify the dead body of Brati. When she was asked to do so none of the family members helped her. She was even denied taking the car to the police station by her husband.

> "I need the car. I'm going to Chaudhuri. You ring up Dutta. Tell him...Why don't you go over straightaway?" (138).

Sujata who is already collapsed emotionally with the news of the death of Brati is even more treated in a bad way by all her family members, deserting her all alone in such a situation. On hearing the news of Brati, Sujata desperately wishes to reach the station to see her son. Both her husband and her son Jyothi behave in a suspicious manner.

As the play moves on, the story is now actually set after two years of the death of Brati. All the family members except Sujata have forgotten about Brati. They don't even remember that such a person existed in their family. Everyone other than Sujata has recovered from Brati's death. They have chosen his birthday, which is also his death day, to celebrate the youngest daughter's engagement, forgetting to mourn the death of Brati, which happened on the same day 2 years ago. Only Sujata lives in the memory of Brati.

Sujata is very much worried that all her family members are against Brati.

> "To Tony and his crowd, to the others, you, your father, Jyothi, Neepa, the way you all speak his name as if Brati was a criminal" (143).

Sujata is not only worried about the death of her son. She is very much worried and emotionally down because of the behaviour of her own family members towards her and towards the dead son. They actually finalise him to be a Naxalite and they treated him in that context both before his death and after his death.

Sujata feels that both she and her son are being alienated within the family because they do not follow the codes of conduct. They are actually being treated as outsiders in their own family. Sujata who couldn't tolerate this expresses her emotions to Nandini when she meets her.

> "With Brati, they have cast me too in the opposite camp" (158).

It is only after the death of her son, Sujata identifies that she herself is being alienated from her family and is kept in isolation. The political awakening in Sujata, happens after her meeting with Somu's mother and Nandhini. The meeting with these two women led Sujata to go in search of the reason behind the death of her loving son, which finally led to the finding of the reason and to the identification of her own self within the family. She is made aware of the difference between the values of our family and her son's ideology.

Her meeting with Somu's mother brought a tremendous change in the mind of Sujata.

> "It was the second time I visited Somu's mother. I didn't know Brati well enough, Somu's mother knew him better. When I visited her I find Brati" (162).

The meeting with Somu's mother made Sujata realise that she is not the only mother to lose her son in the encounter but there are so many like her and her son. The conversations with Nandhini and Somu's mother, lead Sujata to come out of the role of Angel in the house, step out and confront other women and understand the emptiness of her family ideology. Even though Sujata undergoes all these pain within herself, she never shared it with her family members because she was well aware of the fact that none of them were ready to accept what she said especially about Brati. By the end of the play Sujata recognises that she is more than just the mother of Brati, she is a universal mother who mourns the death of many boys like her own son who has been murdered for believing in a different ideology.

The trauma that Sujata undergoes psychologically is presented symbolically through the pain of a swollen appendix. In the final act of the play we find Sujata delivering a monologue. The entire family of Sujata is at Tuli's engagement party. Sujata who is already heartbroken, couldn't tolerate the words uttered by the family and the neighbours regarding Brati's misguided youth and they also blame Sujata for his death. The entry of Saroj Pal, who has been promoted for his heroic action against the naxals, causes the inner conflict of Sujata to burst out.

Sujatha shouts out at the spectators for being involved in the murder of many boys like her own son by remaining silent. In the final act of the play, Sujatha tries to keep the memory of her son and his sacrifice by using all the readers to live and work for the cause. Then she falls down and dies as her appendix bursts.

> "Do the living die only to leave the world to the dead to enjoy? No! Never ! Let this no of mine appears the heart of this city, rise to the skies, be born on the winds, over the whole state, to every nook and corner. Let it set the past, the present and the future a tremble. Let it down the happiness of everyone cooped up in his own happiness" (172).

The play is an awakening of an apolitical mother. It is the death of her son that changes her life. She undergoes various situations where she is being lowered by her own family members under the pretext of her son and his misguided youth. Being the mother of a misguided youth Sujata is also accused of the death of her own son. The unnatural death awakens her to an awareness of her alienation. The quest of the mother to find the truth of her son's death leads her to the discovery of kinship with her son's ideology. Even though there are several situations which awaken the anger in the heart of the mother, she tries to suppress it within herself which finally explodes. The exploding of her emotion, resulted in the worsening of her appendix which led to her death. Thus the paper "The Psychological Conflict Underwent by the Mother in *Mother of 1084*", explains in detail the psychological trauma that Sujata underwent after the death of her son.

Works Cited

Devi, Mahasweta. Trans. Samik Bandopadhyaya "Five Plays", Seagull, Culcutta 1997. print.

Mukherjee, Sujith book rev- "Mahasweta Devi's Writings" June 1991 print.

Annapoorni, S. *South Asian Literature in English*, Mainspring Publishers, 2018.

CHAPTER 9

The Concept of Ostracism: Incessant Trauma in The Lives of LGBT

Monisha M. and Dr. B. Sajeetha

The twentieth century seems far more advanced and developed than the former years in many fields like politics, technology, religious beliefs, economy and many such things. But when it comes to the topic of 'sex' or 'gender', the subject seemed to be troublesome and there are conflicts that raise everyday for equality. The women want equal rights like men, whereas the queer people who are often labeled under the LGBT wants the same rights like the heterosexual people. The queer people are pushed outside the boundaries and they are excluded in everything. The concept of male and female is deeply imprinted and thus the concept of gender binary makes the lives of LGBT people hard and tough. It seems to be a strenuous process for the LGBT to bring equality and to provide them with equal opportunities and egalitarianism. Lesbians, gays, bisexuals, and transgender people are more likely than heterosexuals to face intolerance, discrimination, harassment, and the threat of violence because of their sexual orientation.

The term ostracism means "the act of deliberately not including somebody in a group or activity or the state of not being included" (Oxford Learner's Dictionary). Ostracism poses a serious threat as it excludes and rejects the LGBT in every structure. While the heteronormativity ideas marginalise the Lesbian (L), gay (G) and bisexual (B) people, the gender non-conforming individuals and transgenders (T) are discriminated by the non-binary for their different expressions of gender. The phrase "LGBTQ" refers to a group of people who have experienced various sorts and degrees of trauma. Because of their sexual orientation or gender identity, many

LGBTQ youth feel unsafe in their schools, and some do not feel welcome in their families and communities. LGBTQ youth who are afraid of being rejected by their family may experience stress as a result of concealing their identity. LGBTQ youth face a higher rate of sexual and physical abuse than their straight peers, in addition to the fear of humiliation and alienation.

The term 'ostracism' was derived from the Greek word "ostrakizein" which means "to banish by voting with potsherds" (Merriam Webster). There was a tradition in the Greek law that the citizens of the city were allowed to vote by writing a name of the people they hate in the shards of ceramic pots. The person who got the most votes would be banished from their city for ten years. This method was followed to keep up the peace and to maintain the democracy guarded from the trouble maker. The one who got banished from their hometown would face many outcomes like leaving their home, losing their attachment with their friends and family. Thus the term came into usage with the meaning of excluding someone.

Ostracism can happen to these marginalised people at multiple levels in institution, legal, social and it impacts heavily on the lives of these people. They undergo tortures and pain both physically and mentally, which leads them to depression, stress and suicidal thoughts. Institutional ostracism creates a deep influence in the minds of the young people. When they are ridiculed, mocked, discriminated against for their different expressions of gender, they tend to develop low standards about them and constantly they will be in search of their identity. They are excluded from the circles of friendship, family, community and also in the communication circle.

> In today's society, identity functions to provide coherence to the subject for the purpose of self-presentation to others. In consumerist culture, identity serves the purpose of controlling, commodifying, and marketing the subject... In being, as they must, adopted and acquired through imitation, all identities will fail to satisfy and will be constantly loss, hallmarked by others fragility, and segregate the individual into discrete categories. (Kuzniar 62)

Traumatic events frequently involve a menace to one's life or safety, but any scenario that leaves you feeling overwhelmed and lonely, even if it does not involve physical injury, can cause trauma. The subjective emotional response of the event, not the objective conditions, determines whether or not an incident is traumatic. The more fearful and powerless you feel, the more likely you are to become traumatised. Living in a society where heterosexuality is typically portrayed as the only appropriate orientation and homosexuality is considered as abnormal, lesbian, gay, bisexual, and transgender (LGBT) people confront enormous challenges. They continue to experience discrimination and marginalisation in all aspects of life around the world.

LGBTQ youth are more likely than the straight peers to face problems that can undermine resilience, such as a higher chance of traumatic stress exposure, a lack of adult support or affirming communities, and a lack of control over external conditions and responses. LGBTQ youth are more likely to develop depression, post-traumatic stress disorder, suicide-related behaviors, substance addiction, HIV, and relationship problems as a result of discrimination, violence, and lack of support or rejection from caregivers, peers, and communities. Homophobic violence and abuse against LGBT individuals are frequent. The problems and the legal cases of the LGBTQ are not taken very seriously. Even when the government has created a few laws and acts for the welfare of these people, they are not in use in most of the cases. The LGBT people are prevented to get equality in the jurisdictions regarding sexual orientations as well as gender identity in their non-discrimination ordinances. It emotionally and physically suppresses and excludes these people from their basic rights.

> Same-sex couples understood their status under these laws to be that of "second-class citizens" excluded from the beliefs, protections, rights, and responsibilities of the civil institution of marriage. These laws also excluded them from the social acceptance or legitimacy of civil marriage. Thus, these relationships were ostracized by the political system.... These laws explicitly proscribe discrimination, or differential treatments, that act to exclude individuals from certain groups from common privileges. (Riggle 6)

At the individual, interpersonal, and societal levels, marginalisation is at the root of restriction from satisfying the social lives. People on the margins have little control over the situation and the resources available to them; they are often stigmatised and are frequently the target of negative public opinions. Their chances to contribute to society may be constrained, and they may acquire low self-esteem and lack of self-confidence, as they grow isolated. They have inadequate access to valuable social resources such as education and health services, housing, income, leisure activities, and jobs as a result of social policies and practices.

Even in the present advanced contemporary society, many people would consider transgender to be a mental illness. They are deeply considered as deep-seated psychopathologists, who mutilate their body and oppose the sexual stereotypes. They're rumored to be sick. The research suggests that people in the transgender community are viewed simply as a mental disorder to be diagnosed and treated by trained medical practitioners. They undergo painful surgery that will help them get rid of their pain for a lifetime. The public never tries to understand the trauma the trans people experience, when they feel trapped in a wrong body.

The thought and fear of exclusion in the family gatherings because of their gay, lesbian, bisexual or transgender identity would result in the social ostracism. It acts through ignoring someone because of their gender non-conforming identity and treating those people like the silenced or shunning them like they don't exist. For example, a gay won't be called for the peer group party; lesbian daughter would be treated differently by her family. A trans woman will be totally avoided by her co-workers. Social ostracism isolates and separates them as the prey of ostracism. Their expression of gender or sexuality outside the norms makes them excluded, ostracised and thus they are not accepted and belonged with the dominant cisgender groups.

> For humans, ostracism over a long period of time is a form of social death. In the short term, however, there are several ways in which a person might counter such a threat: by attempting to rescue his or her place in the group, trying to regain control that has been lost, or striking back by lashing out in some way. The social pain created by ostracism and the change in affect can both alert individuals to focus on the ostracism episode and to reflect on its meaning. (Williams 72)

Discrimination against LGBTQ people occurs in a range of situations and settings, including the workplace and places of worship. When compared to their gender-conforming peers, LGBTQ people are typically denied career advancement or equal pay, and their unemployment rate is twice that of the general population. Religious institutions respond to LGBTQ individuals in a variety of ways, ranging from unequivocal support to outright rejection. The rejection or condemnation of homosexuality and non-binary gender identities can be extremely traumatising for LGBTQ people who grow up in otherwise friendly environments. Thus, LGBT people have been marginalised and they experience prejudice either consciously or unconsciously.

Social ostracism damages the individuals so hard and it creates greater harm to these people. Likewise, when they are rejected by their family, it impacts heavily more than being ostracised by an unknown person. When these people are excluded and chased away from their family, they undergo trauma and pain which will often lead them to unwanted thoughts like suicidal temptations. When they are chased away or when they come out of their home voluntarily, they are in need of money to satisfy their daily needs. Thus the LGBT people, in order to satisfy their daily needs they will involve themselves in prostitution and other sex works like stripping, online prostitution and some will indulge in criminal activities.

Trauma experienced as a child can have serious and long-term consequences. When childhood trauma is not addressed, an adult's experience of fear and powerlessness persists, setting the groundwork for future trauma. Even if the trauma had occurred many years ago, there are measures to be taken to conquer the suffering, reclaim the level of psychological stability, and learn to trust and connect with others again. The idea of social stress relies on stress theory by arguing that situations in the social environment, rather than only personal events, can cause mental and bodily harm. As a result, those who belong to stigmatised social groups, such as socioeconomic class, race/ethnicity, gender, or sexuality, might expect social stress to have a significant influence on their life.

LGBT people are considered to be a great threat to the gender and sexual identity, behavioral norms of the heteronormative binary culture because of their non-conforming gender issues. The LGBT people would definitely face ostracism in their lifetime, from institutional to social context. Political ostracism happens through the legal forms and social ostracism occurs through the exclusion in the interpersonal and group interactions. Focusing on the seriousness of the ostracism, they posit risks and harms because of the internalisation, discrimination, distress and prejudice.

> Due to the lack of widespread legitimate recognition in the area of the LGBT+ Community, oftentimes the members of the same are resolutely ignored and, in most cases, alienated. They are considered no longer a ratified member of the society and their uniqueness is interpreted in the likes of a contagious virus. Henceforth, they take the form of 'The Other'; the ones who are 'abnormal'. (Srivastava)

Ostracism threatens the LGBT people and they are removed from the concept of gender binary from social acceptance. These people undergo pain both emotionally and physically. It acts as a social act that creates a serious risk to physical health and psychological well-being. The physical pain can't be just the abuse and the physical tortures; it also includes the pain they get through the Sexually Transmitted Diseases (STD). When they indulge in sexual activities or prostitution, the chance of getting the STD diseases like AIDS, syphilis are high and thus they will be affected terribly. This pain reduces self-esteem, and results in the thought of helplessness, alienation, worthlessness, discrimination, alcohol usage, drug abuse and also the suicidal tendencies.

It is undeniable that LGBT people, who are defined by their sexual orientation, endure prejudice and exclusion from society, and hence frequently confront challenges in meeting their requirements. This isolation and ostracism can range from simple personal relationships to the most widespread social ignorance, restriction, ostracism, operating in tandem, and can even be a violation of human rights. Lesbians, gay men, bisexuals, and transgender persons have long been active in racial and economic justice movements and most of the people from that community have a similar kind of journey which is filled and characterised by pain, atrocities, discrimination, prejudice, stigma, and also the state of being ostracised. Ostracism is used as a tool by the cisgender and heteronormative people which is used against the queer people. This small thin lining ties all of the LGBT people together to become a strong community under the term queer. These people should be considered as human beings, rather than thinking them to be marginalised or untouchables, and they should be treated equally like other people.

The pain and sufferings are inexpressible and often their voices are denied and unheard because they are different from the expressions of the gender binary. "The collective burden of alienation and ostracism on the shoulders of the nonconforming dissenters, otherwise known as the LGBT community, are indelibly illustrative of emotional trauma which is further exacerbated through internalised queer phobia and throes of gender dysphoria" (Srivastava). Ostracism focuses on the human needs and they clearly portray the stigmatisation of the LGBT. Therefore, ostracism acts as an essential factor for understanding the distress, pain, suffering and also the hardened plight of the LGBT. Today, LGBT organisers and groups are progressively drawing parallels between the LGBT rights movement and the socio- economic justice movements, pointing out that these people have multi-layered personalities and identities, and are members of multiple communities experiencing oppression and privilege.

The identity of the LGBT can be turned into a positive one with "feeling authentic, a sense of belonging and community connection, having satisfying intimate relationships, self-awareness and insight, and a commitment to and involvement in social justice and compassion" (Riggle 19). The individuals with the LGBT identity will have the risk of experiencing prejudice whether they disclose their identity or not. The LGBT identity should be considered seriously and they should be allowed to make their own choices about the disclosure and concealment of their identity. A support system should be constructed for dealing with the harms of ostracism. It should be able to provide a sense of belonging where the lives of LGBT will be improved to live a good life. Society must be taught to stop judging a person by looking at their outward appearance and hence the expectations of the binary cisgender and heterosexuality can be broken. In order to bring equality to these people, it is not only the responsibility of the cisgender people, but it is also the responsibility of the judicial law systems too. They can be visible and that they will be considered as normal in the society.

Works Cited

Kuzniar, Alice A. "Identity Precarious Sexualities: Queer Challenges to Psychoanalytic and Social Identity Categorisation." *Clinical Encounters in Sexuality: Psychoanalytic Practice and Queer Theory,* 2017, JSTOR.

"Ostracism." *Oxford Learner's Dictionary*, https://www.oxfordlearnersdictionaries.com/definition/english/ostracism.

"Ostracize." *Merriam Webster*, https://www.merriam-webster.com/dictionary/ostracize.

Riggle, Ellen. "Ostracism as a framework for understanding LGBT well-being and risk." *ResearchGate*, Apr 2018, www.researchgate.net/publication/324827136_Ostracism_as_a_framework_for_understanding_LGBT_well-being_and_risk.

Srivastava, Aakshi. "Alienation And Ostracism: Two Reasons Why Reception Of Queer Community Is Still Stagnant." *Gaysi*, 15 June 2020, gaysifamily.com/2020/06/15/alienation-and-ostracism-two-reasons-why-reception-of-queer-community-is-still-stagnant/.

Williams, Kipling D., and Steve A Nida. "Ostracism: Consequences and Coping." *Association for Psychological Science*, vol. 20, no. 2, Apr 2011. *ResearchGate*, researchgate.net/publication/254081778_Ostracism_Consequences_and_Coping.

CHAPTER 10

Cross-Cultural Aspects of Africana Womanism: A Philosophical Overview

Nayana. N.V

Culture consists of the beliefs, behaviours, objects, and other characteristics common to the members of a particular group or society. Through culture, people and groups define themselves, conform to society's shared values, and contribute to society. Thus, culture includes many societal aspects: language, customs, values, norms, mores, rules, tools, technologies, products, organisations, and institutions. This latter term institution refers to clusters of rules and cultural meanings associated with specific social activities. Common institutions are the family, education, religion, work, and health care. Sociologists define society as the people who interact in such a way as to share a common culture. The cultural bond may be ethnic or racial, based on gender, or due to shared beliefs, values, and activities. The term *society* can also have a *geographic* meaning and refer to people who share a common culture in a particular location. For example, people living in arctic climates developed different cultures from those living in desert cultures. In time, a large variety of human cultures arose around the world.

Africana womanism is a term coined in the late 1980s by Clenora Hudson-Weems. It is intended as an ideology applicable to all women of African descent. It is grounded in African culture and Afrocentrism and focuses on the experiences, struggles, needs, and desires of Africana women of the African diaspora. It distinguishes itself from Feminism, or Alice Walker‘s Womanism. Africana womanism pays more attentionand focuses more on the realities and the injustices in society in regard to race. Hudson-Weems sought to create an ideology specific to African women and women of African descent. Hudson-Weems believes that the creation of the ideology separates African women's accomplishments from African male scholars, feminism, and Black feminism. Hudson-Weems argues that Africana womanism is not an addendum to feminism, Black feminism, African feminism, or Alice Walker's Womanism. Feminism and gender issues are separate entities that are not reliant upon each other, and therefore, Africana women are able to address gender issues without partaking in feminist activity.

Africana Womanism Society lists 18 characteristics 18 key components that form Africana womanism. The characteristics include Self-Naming, Self-Definition, Family-Centeredness, Wholeness, Role Flexibility, Adaptability, Authenticity, Black Female Sisterhood, Struggling with males against oppression, Male Compatibility, Recognition, Ambition, Nurturing, Strengthen, Respect, Respect for Elders, Mothering, and Spirituality. African men and women do not accept the ideology of feminism. There is a general consensus in the Africana community that the feminist movement, by and large, is the white woman's movement for two reasons. First, the Africana woman does not see the man as her primary enemy as does the white feminist, who is carrying out an age-old battle with her white male counterpart for subjugating her as his property. Africana men have never had the same institutionalised power to oppress Africana women as white men have had to oppress white women. Africana womanism contrasts a racist and sexist feminist/womanist ideology, and many Africana women (and men) have come to embrace it. Africana womanist ideology contributes to Afrocentric discourse. The fundamental foundation of Africana womanism is built on traditional Africana philosophy and values and on Afrocentric theories. Some of the traditional values forefront the role of African mothers as leaders in the struggle to regain, reconstruct, and create a cultural integrity that espouses the ancient Maatic principles of reciprocity, balance, harmony, justice, truth, righteousness, order, and so forth.

The first principle Self-Naming discusses the importance of self-identifying as an African woman in society. The Africana identification is distinguishable from feminism and Black variants. Self-naming is the period of recognising the need for an Africana movement with its own name. The second principle defined, Self-Definition, begins to describe realities that African women face, through a Pan-African lens. The Pan-African movement attempts to create a sense of brotherhood among all people of African descent, regardless of whether or not they live on the continent of Africa. Self-definition explores gender inequalities and stereotypes in the modern patriarchy. Self-naming and self-definition are the first two couple of characteristics of Africana womanism. The term "nommo" is given to the idea of self-naming, which is important because in order for one to exist it has to be given a correct name. There is an increasing need for self-naming, self-defining, and self-identity for Black people and self-defining helps to discover one's identity through personal point of view of their world that goes against that of the dominant culture.

The second groupings of characteristics are family-centeredness, wholeness, authenticity, role flexibility, adaptability, struggle with Black men against oppression, and Black female sisterhood. The second grouping of characteristics includes Family-Centeredness, Wholeness, Authenticity, Role Flexibility, Adaptability, in connection with men and Genuine Sisterhood. The principle of family-centeredness focuses on the entire black family unit. The interest in the success of the black community as a whole maintains a sense of wholeness. Any important outcomes are shared as overarching closeness of the Black community that is enforced by the women in society. The third and last clustering of characteristics are strength, male compatibility, respect, recognition, respect for elders, ambition, mothering, nurturing, and spirituality. Historically, Black women always had psychological and physical strength especially with what happened with slavery. Hudson-Weems says that Black men's and Black women's bond helps to maintain the race. Black woman are physically and mentally strong. This principle of Strength is often the one that is attacked by non-Africana oppressors because their goal is to force submission upon the powerful group that is Africana women. Hudson-Weems says that Black men's and Black women's bond helps to maintain the race. Therefore, the principle of male compatibility is based upon mutually beneficial relationships between a well-respected African woman and a supportive, like-minded, man.

Respect and recognition go together that is necessary for a healthy respect for Africana womanists. It helps them relate to others. Respect and recognition also contribute to the self-love and admiration and to the respect for elders or older members in the Black community. To dissect both principles a bit further, respect refers to reverence an African woman has for herself, absent of the colonised standards. Determining one's worth while ignoring politics, is crucial to becoming a confident African woman. The pillar of Recognition refers to the acknowledgement of humanity, capability, and power of Black women. Recognition plays a large role in keeping communal peace and ensuring the Black women's effectiveness in the struggle for equality. The principles that outline the caring nature of the Africana womanist are defined below. Respect for Elders, is an extension of the historical African tradition of ancestral reverence. Ancestral reverence is the habitual act of caring for elders, and eventual ancestors, within a community or society. Once the elders become ancestors, they will be responsible for providing wisdom and guidance which is highly vauled. The Nurturer and Mother are both described as a call for all community members to play an active role in the rearing of the community and as a propaganda of race through care. It is an African woman's duty to not only care and nourish her family, but to provide the care and nourishment for her race as a whole. By fostering and guiding fellow women, the Africana Movement is advanced. There is an initiative for public's appreciation and education about the Africana Movement that exemplifies the principle of Ambition.

The final principle is Spirituality, which stresses the importance of the reverence for traditional African spiritual systems. These spiritual systems call for a collection of the principles including Ancestral Reverence, Oneness with oneself, and with nature as well. Africana womanist is also very spiritual and believe in a higher power and the mothering and nurturing is traditional.

Works Cited

"Africana Womanism: The Flip Side of a Coin," in *The Western Journal of Black Studies*, 2001.

"Africana Womanism: An Overview," in *Out of the Revolution: The Development of Africana Studies*, Delores Aldridge and Carlene Young, Editors, Lexington Books, 2000, pp. 205-217.

Hudson-Weems, C. 2008. *Africana Womanism & Race & Gender in the Presidential Candidacy of Barack Obama.* Authorhouse, ISBN 1-4389-0906-3,

Hudson-Weems, C, 2004. *Africana Womanist Literary Theory.* Trenton: Africa World Press

"Theorising difference within black feminist thought: The dilemma of sexism in black communities", Austin, Algernon. Race, Gender & Class New Orleans: July 31, 1999. Vol. 6, Issue 3; p. 52.

CHAPTER 11

Encapsulation of Traumatic Experiences: A Reading of Peter Handke's *Repetition*

Neethu A. Nair and Dr. N. U. Lekshmi

> "Psychic Trauma occurs when a sudden, unexpected, overwhelming intense emotional blow or a series of blows assaults the person from outside. Traumatic events are external, but they quickly become incorporated into the mind."
>
> Lenore Terr

Trauma theory emerges as an intense fright that pulls down one's identity. It is an interdisciplinary field of study developed in the 1990s. Trauma is a word that disrupts the lives of humans. It is the cross-fertilisation of psychology and humanities. The theory emerges due to the after-effects of the Holocaust of World War II. It plays a very important role in various fields like psychiatry, sociology, humanities, film studies, literature, and psychoanalysis. The representations in language, shaping the individuals through memory, cultural identities are the main elements that trauma studies investigate. The theoretical foundation later relied on Freudian principles to develop a model of trauma. Splitting of the ego and dissociation harbored inside the unconscious is defined as trauma. A traumatic experience is an interplay between the external and internal forces of an individual. The most prominent figures in the field of trauma theory are Kali Tal and Cathy Caruth. The writers try to portray the inner conflicts of mind through the medium of literature. The haunting of the mind mainly through memory is well expressed in terms of 'repressed memory' by Freud. The main problem faced by the characters is their failure to find out their own identity in society. So there is a need to expose the traumatic narratives which can be possible only through different genres of literature. Peter

Handke, a well-known German writer and a Nobel Prize winner through his novel "Repetition" depicts the disordered psyche of the narrator using the technique of stream of consciousness. The paper tries to bring forth the story of an Austrian, of mixed German and Slovenian heritage, who goes to communist Yugoslavia in a search for identity. It is a novel about alienation and a feeling of being at home and lost in the world. It searches the past to make the present understandable and prepare a clear way to the future. It is a story of paradise lost, and then regained. It is mentioned as a laborious journey through life, within the self, within the community as a predator and prey that finally results in detachment.

A study of trauma in Peter Handke's *Repetition* directs back to the narrator's young age. The narrator uses the stream of consciousness technique to intensify the reading experience. The novel depicts a 45-year-old narrator who recalls a trip from Carinthia to Slovenia in search of his brother, Gregor. He is armed with two of Gregor's books: a copybook from agricultural school and a Slovenian – German dictionary in which Gregor has marked certain words. The traceless disappearance of his brother in the Second World War also symbolises how cruel circumstances curtail human beings. The departure for the imaginary true homeland, lying across the mountains, is an attempt at self-liberation.

Memory plays a prominent role in this novel. The narrator's thoughts shatter between the past and the present through memories. He renames memories as reminiscences of the fragile mind. The narrator recounts his childhood and a journey he undertakes into the Slovenian part when he was twenty. He and his family stay on the border of Yugoslavia. His father is one of a devout and hardworking stock of Slovene journeymen. His Mother is non-Slovene, godless, blasphemous, who expects salvation only from the hard work. Filip encounters a detachment from the rest of the villagers. His family background makes a big impact on him. His sister Ursula is mentally disturbed and Gregor elopes to Yugoslavia. His mother thinks that he has joined the partisans but Filip thinks that he has just gone into Yugoslavia for higher studies. In the end, Filip convinces that he just wants to narrate his own story rather than finding his brother. Much of his life is mundane by saying

> What I had experienced at the age of twenty was not yet a memory. And memory meant not that what-had-been situated itself by recurring, but that what-had-been situated itself by recurring. If I remembered, it first became known to me, nameable, voiced, speakable; accordingly I look on memory as more than haphazard thinking back-as work; the work of memory situates experience in a sequence that keeps it alive, a story which can open out into free storytelling, greater life, invention. (63)

The traumatic fear makes every character in the novel search for an exit from the world. The story begins with a talk between Filip and a border guard. He makes him understand that the meaning of the word 'Kobal' which suggests the span between parted legs, and a person standing with legs outspread. The hopes of the Kobal family in search of their son and waiting for his return are reflected in all aspects of the novel. The family's favorite word 'holy' is referred not to the church, but to everyday life activities. But they have a wishful dream of their son's return home. A strong self-assurance of the exile is represented in the character of the Kobal family. Filip Kobal self-assured the imposed destiny of the exile as a mark of honor. He considers himself as self-reliant, bold, rebellious, and independent and boasts as other man's hero. According to family mythology, the Kobals are the designated representatives of the Slovenian people. They are powerless people without aristocracy, military marches, and land of their own. They always remain uncorrupted. It is not surprising that he has developed solitary habits. This shows his alienation from the family. As an illustration of not joining his classmates on their trip to Greece, he sets out alone for Slovenia, his ancestral homeland where his brother disappears.

> I had got used, during the past year, to my class in the state school in Klagenfurt, where girls were in the majority, and now I suddenly found myself alone. While my classmates piled into the bus together and set out for Greece, I played the loner who preferred to go to Yugoslavia by himself. (3)

The childhood experiences of the narrator intensify the narrator's trauma in many ways. The distressing experiences pollute his good days. In his first school, he is harassed by his fellow boys from neighboring village and an enemy from his own village. His second school is a seminary where he feels homesick because of the enmity towards his teacher. The third school is the gymnasium in the nearby town of Klagenfurt where he stands out as an awkward country boy among the glib city teenagers.

> The only good company I had at the seminary I enjoyed alone when studying. In my solitary study, every word I remembered, every formula I applied correctly, every watercourse I learned to draw from memory, anticipated my one overriding desire: to be out in the open. If asked what the word 'kingdom' meant to me, I would not have named any particular country but only the 'Kingdom of freedom'. (19)

The harrowing effects of trauma can be traced in children through cultural marginality. It refers to experiences of individuals living within cultures but integrated into neither of them. Filip's father is an example of cultural marginalisation by marrying an Austrian woman. He encourages the same identification in their sons, Gregor and Filip. This marginality affects them socially and psychologically. This divided culture explains unhappiness in public and at home. It is perceived throughout the novel.

Repetition is not a sad story of unsuccessful struggle and banishment, but an attestation of the family's aim and aspiration as a promise. This is the view of his mother. She demands it from her inner self. His father believes in God and blindly accepts the role of destiny in life. The mother's law decreed her family and she claims the efforts to build a home on the other side of the Karawanken Mountains someday. This Austrian woman is an expression of supreme contempt in the Isonzo valley. The narrator's family usually argues in the name of God. A map of Slovenia is hung at the entrance. She used to chant names from the map syllable after syllable on a high note. Her pronunciation is faulty but sounded beautiful to him. His mother never crosses the border and the Yugoslavia towns are known to her from her husband's story. This shows her inner dilemma of not having an identity of her own and longs for existential individuality.

Mental trauma focuses on the visualisation of old personal memories. There is a comparison of traumatic mind to the skin of a snake. It symbolises looking at the past: the lost parts of oneself in order to understand former selves by describing the discarded skins left on the path. The lost members of the family are like the skin of the snake. The terrible traumatic experience of the narrator is depicted through wild dreams. The narrator's waking moments are bright and dreams are dark. They banish the narrator from his supposed paradise and flung him into hell. He is the damned and the tormentor in all sense. He is afraid of falling asleep. His guilt at not being at home with his people figured in every dream. He usually sees his home, but not a human being in it. The house is in ruin. The roof is caved in and the garden is full of weeds and jumping snakes.

> The first night in a foreign country might perhaps be told briefly, but in my memory, it has become the longest in my life, decades-long. At the age of twenty, I wouldn't have dreamed of stopping at a hotel-and not only because I wanted to save money. Yet my only thought was sleep, and the tunnel did not strike me as an insane idea. I would go in where my train had just carried me out. All that mattered was a niche to sleep in. (66)

The characters in the novel experience mental estrangements in life. At the end of the story, the narrator believes in the salvation of one's fragile mind. Handke concludes the novel in a religious perspective. Everyone can be purified through prayers. Many mental disorders and disorderliness of the mind, find liberation through chanting. Peter Handke succeeds in saving his characters from traumatic fears and finds root in their existence. The novel ends up with a prayer and Filip discovers the transformative power of the language to describe the world. He experiences the unnerving joy of being an outsider in a strange world. The novel makes a great and lasting impression on everyone who reads and ends with a prayer.

> King, Child, get hold of yourself, sit up straight, prop yourself on your elbows, smile all around you, take a deep breath, and start all over again with your all-appeasing And then...(216)

Works Cited

Caruth Cathy. *Unclaimed Experience: Trauma,* Narrative, and History. Hopkins UP, 1996.

LaCapra, Dominick. *Writing History, Writing Trauma.* Hopkins UP, 2001.

Manheim, Ralph. *Repetition.* Trans. Peter Handke, USA, 1988.

Terr, L.C. *Too Scared to Cry: Psychic Trauma in Childhood.* New York, 1990.

CHAPTER 12

The Myth of Returning Home: *Sea Prayer* as a Narrative of Refugee Trauma

Rajasree R.

In August 2015, a photographic image caught the attention of the world. It was the picture of two-year old Alan Kurdi's dead body drowned in the Mediterranean Sea and washed ashore; his body lying face down on the beach. He was a Kurdish child from Syria who had been flying the Syrian civil war with his parents and was drowned in the Mediterranean Sea. Alan and his family were Syrian refugees and they were trying to reach Europe when their boat capsized and he drowned to death along with his mother and a brother. "The image and his name quickly became synonymous with one of the many catastrophes of the twenty-first century: the refugee crisis" (Ballengee and Kelman 141).

Fig. 1 Image of Alan Kurdi at the Mediterranean after he drowned on 2 September 2015

Though Globalisation and developments in Science and Technology seemingly claim to have created a borderless world, the reality is different. The World hasn't transcended borders but has created stronger boundaries making it more difficult even to move or relocate. Migrants are dying each day while crossing borders or while fleeing from violence, war or persecution; they are no more migrants but refugees.

The image of the drowned Syrian boy echoed the trauma of the migrants who had to shift from "home as the world" to having to "feel at home in the world" (145). Alan Kurdi's body at some beach in Turkey, "which was neither his home nor where he was headed" reveal the grave reality of being "homeless" (145).

Khaled Hosseini, the Afghan-American novelist has written the *Sea Prayer* (2018) inspired by the story of Alan Kurdi. Hosseini and his family had relocated and later sought political asylum in the United States due to the continuous civil war and the atrocities that followed in his homeland Afghanistan. In 2006, Khaled was appointed a Goodwill Ambassador for UNHCR, the UN Refugee Agency. He later established 'The Khaled Hosseini Foundation', a non-profit organisation which provides humanitarian assistance to the people of Afghanistan. (*Khaled Hosseini*)

Hosseini is an established author with the theme of migration predominant in all his novels. His *Sea Prayer* is a short poetic work, a poignant one with illustrations by Dan Williams. In the blurb to the text, he states "In the year after Alan's death, 4176 others died or went missing attempting that same journey." Hosseini, being the goodwill ambassador of UNHCR, United Nations' Refugee Agency and himself being a refugee from Afghanistan, was shattered by the photograph of the drowned boy. Hosseini's *Sea Prayer* is a heart touching story poetically written as a letter by a father to his son awaiting rescue. The fear, anxiety and helplessness of a Syrian refugee is poignantly portrayed by the author. He has dedicated the book "to the thousands of refugees who have perished at sea fleeing war and persecution" (Introduction).

The American Psychiatric Association described traumatic events as "outside the range of usual human experience" in 1980 (qtd. in *Trauma and Recovery* 33) but traumatic events are more so due to the extremities of helplessness and terror that they evoke the responses of catastrophe. The *Comprehensive Textbook of Psychiatry* defines the common denominator of psychological trauma as the feeling of "intense fear, helplessness, loss of control, and threat of annihilation" (33). The refugees suffer from the trauma of multiple losses and the past memories come back to them as flashbacks, nightmares and daydreams. The insecurity that they do not fully belong anywhere resist them from being a citizen and they remain refugees.

Sea Prayer is the prayer of every refugee parent who holds their younger ones closest to them uncertain how long they all would survive. Next moment or so, they would never be seeing each other again. On a moonlit beach, the father carries his sleeping son and waits for the boat to arrive. Along with a few others, they are about to risk a perilous voyage across the sea in search of a new home. The narrator talks his thoughts aloud, as if addressing his son though he is deep asleep. He recalls how as a child he has spent a peaceful summer at his grandfather's house, the images that he reflects portray a life impossible even to dream of.

"My dear Marwan", he says

"in the long summers of childhood,
when I was the boy the age you are now,
your uncles and I
spread our mattress on the roof
of your grandfather's farmhouse
outside of Homs" (1).

Hiding the pain within, he describes the sights and sounds of a peaceful rustic life, his home-town Homs in Syria: the breeze stirring the olive trees, bleating of grandmother's goats and the clanking of her cooking pots (2). The narrator refers to his wife who has become a memory. About her he says: "I have a sharply etched memory of your mother from that trip" (3). Death of his wife conveys the trauma of multiple losses of the narrator. He says: "You have learned that mothers and sisters and classmates can be found in narrow gaps between concrete, bricks and exposed beams, little patches of sunlit skin shining in the dark" (12). Rape, violence and sexual exploitation, refugee women suffer myriad atrocities. His wife has become a martyr amidst the abuses by the military against the civilians. Life was not safe for anyone in Syria anymore. His beautiful hometown is now a deadly war zone. Hossieni speaks about how the memories of one's homeland has turned to mere memory "But that life, that time, seems like a dream now, even to me, like some long-dissolved rumour" (*Sea Prayer* 7). Witnessing "protests, siege, the skies spitting bombs, starvation, burials", he says to his son "These are the things you know" (8-9); only traumatic events await a refugee.

Fig. 2 *Sea Prayer* as a tribute to the refugees perished at sea

The mishaps that they have endured and the imminent ones that would befall them have equipped them to look into the barbarous acts of violence. He says: "You know a bomb crater can be made into a swimming hole. You have learned dark blood is better news than bright" (11).

"I have heard it said we are the uninvited. We are the unwelcome. We should take our misfortune elsewhere" (13). Other nations do not take in refugees to provide them a shelter/ asylum. Around the world, migrants and refugees are stranded between closed borders. The national/ international policies of each country differ and hence has imposed limits to being hosts to refugees. Refugees are often categorised not as an individual with rights and a moral claim but as the invasive other. (qtd. in Baak 56). He explains how the visual, political and discursive fields operate to construct frames that position refugees not only as Other, but as a threatening undesired Other.

Without proper food, water or shelter, they wait endlessly at the shore for a journey across. "All of us impatient for sunrise, all of us in dread of it. All of us in search of home" (13). The helplessness as a parent unable to protect their own kids is pathetic. Losing the security and shelter of a home, a refugee is forced to live in any part of the world they end up.

> I wish you hadn't been so young.
> You wouldn't have forgotten the farmhouse,
> the soot of its stone walls,
> the creek where your uncles and I built
> a thousand boyhood dams. (4)

The narrator carry fragmented memories of a nostalgic home and a normal childhood his son was blessed to experience at least for a short span of time and lives on through the disaster.

Refugees undergo the trauma of near death experiences and an array of catastrophic events. They struggle to survive over the trauma of displacement and dislocation each moment. Refugee trauma, related to terrible experiences like torture, rape and abuse, fear of displacement, fear of loss of life, livelihood and property is unfathomable. Parents who have suffered devastating losses with their children dead blame themselves for being helpless and powerless. They survive with the guilt that they were unable to protect their own offspring. They undergo a pathetic situation wishing themselves to be dead than being in a half alive situation when someone dear to them were chosen to die instead of them.

The narrator asks his son to hold his hand and assures him nothing bad will happen. He then realises those words are just words, a helpless father's tricks. "How helpless I am to protect you" from the vast, deep, and indifferent sea. (16) And he says all he can do is to pray that they reach ashore safe and secure: the prayer of a thousand refugees around different parts across the world.

With the aftermath of catastrophic events, life is never normal for refugees. They are often forced to migrate without choice and is forced to adjust with the new milieu wherever they end up. The emotional trauma such refugees suffer are difficult to communicate. Haunting memories of traumatic events are recollected and perpetuated across generations, mediated by narratives. As Marianne Hirsch speaks about the generation of 'Postmemory' which is the powerful transmission of the personal, collective and cultural trauma to the generations that follow the survivors. Unlike a lived experience, postmemory is mediated but conveys the pain, knowledge and the impact the trauma has made on the victim. *Sea Prayer* communicates and connects this pain of the refugees not as recollection but as a retelling/ recreation of the event of their collective past.

Global Increase in Forced Displacements

Jennifer Ballengee in her article "Phantom Work" describes the plight of thousands of refugees who suffer displacement and impoverishment and helplessly succumb to death. "By June 2019, there were over 70 million forcibly displaced people in the world – the highest number ever on record. Over 25 million of these people were recognised by the United Nations as refugees of war (217). And UNHCR has recorded that the number rose by 5 million in the years 2016-2019 alone (224). Ballengee notes how less prosperous countries are hosting more refugees per capita than the countries of Europe. "In Greece specifically, over one million migrants and refugees arrived from Syria and other areas of conflict in the fourteen months between January 2015 and March 20, 2016" (218). It was when the European Union agreement with Turkey was signed by which Europe closed its borders agreeing that the migrants from Greece to Turkey would be returned to Turkey. Over 57,000 refugees were stranded in Greece when the borders closed in 2016. And the number had risen to 120,000 refugees and migrants within Greek borders by March 2020, according to the UNHCR. (218).

These people wandered all day, slept under trees at night, others lived in makeshift camps, crowded in official detention camps, in warehouses, tents and in abandoned stadiums. Fleeing war and persecution, hoping against hope, they dare to voyage across the sea in makeshift rafts and small boats and they perish at sea. Many of them leave with only the belongings they can carry along, and are separated by their family members most often losing them to disease, exhaustion or natural calamity. Witnessing the death of closed ones, they travel with the trauma and are often victimised by the authorities. Shattered to the core, it is difficult to rebuild the life of a refugee. According to the International Organisation for Migration (IOM), over 20,000 refugees and migrants have died (primarily from drowning) in attempts to cross the Mediterranean since 2014 as recorded in the 'Missing Migrants Project' (Ballengee and Kelman 219). Those people fleeing from violence, persecution and disaster from their native land face enormous threats on their journey to safety. Afghans, Somalis, Iraqis, Eritreans and Syrians all look forward to a place of refuge.

Ballengee notes a shift in terminology by media after the death of Alan Kurdi. When the journalistic photos of the drowned Kurdi emerged, "it gave a sympathetic human face to the crisis of mass movement" and that it was around this image event that the word "refugee" began to replace "migrants" in media reports. (218)

Kurdi's incident throws light to the exploitive practices of human smugglers who exploit the desperate migrants, they pack these refugees for a perilous journey in small boats and rafts charging huge sums of money. Kurdi's family also faced a similar tragedy. Sixteen people were in the boat which was designed for a maximum of eight people, and they were wearing life jackets which were 'fake' (*Alan Kurdi*).

In Search of a Home outside Homeland

Separated from home and near ones, resettling in a new place, assimilating new culture and adapting to the new society, a refugee is always at a sense of loss, alienation and insecurity. They do not belong anywhere and their identity is labelled as a refugee forever. Losing one's home is losing one's identity. With the loss of neighbourhood, the sense of togetherness as a community is lost. They struggle to maintain a livelihood and most often lack access to proper healthcare and education.

Only very few of the refugees return to their homeland. Though most of them desire for a return, the situations that await them at their homeland are most often not conducive for the same. They wait for a peaceful atmosphere to be restored for their return and that is rare. Humanitarian assistance from UNHCR, national and international agencies strive hard to help the refugees resettle or return. But the practical difficulties are many. Some migrants carry the concept of home and homeland which their parents had once left forever. Most of them wouldn't have visited the land ever in their life, it is the homeland of their parents which they too consider nostalgic. Some others consider their place of living and livelihood as home. Some consider home in terms of relations when their relatives remain back at homeland, but they are stranded elsewhere.

UNHCR reported "with millions of people already forced to flee from their homes and many thousands dying while trying to get to safety, the global humanitarian system has been severely stretched." And that "UNHCR has received information of over 3,500 women, men and children reported dead or missing in the Mediterranean Sea during the year, clearly demonstrating how dangerous and unpredictable this situation has become" ("Global Trends" 2014). The report also analyses how the war in the Syrian Arab Republic entering into the fourth year in 2014 was a major cause in the global increase of forced displacements. "With at least 7.6 million Syrians estimated to be displaced within their country at year end, global forced displacement levels were heavily impacted with this one country. Globally, one in every five displaced persons worldwide was Syrian. The country also became the world's largest source country of refugees during 2014, overtaking Afghanistan, which had held this position for more than 30 years" ("Global Trends" 2014).

New UNHCR estimates show that among refugees and Venezuelans displaced abroad, almost one million children were born in displacement between 2018 and 2020, an average of between 2,90,000 and 3,40,000 per year. Many of them are at risk of remaining in exile for years to come, some potentially for the rest of their lives. ("Global Trends" 2020)

Resuming Lives beyond Borders

Every citizen has the right to life, right to equality and freedom. Beyond borders, these rights are fundamental and universal. But the refugee children are not even granted basic amenities, with their health, safety and education at stake. Global Refugee Forum and asylum laws have been implemented to safeguard them and to promote their access to protection and asylum. Adequate protection from sexual abuse/ violence and timely access to medical services should be ensured to the survivors.

Refugee resettlement has to be undertaken by the host countries. While the number of resettled refugees are only a very few percentage of the total number of displaced people globally, COVID 19 pandemic has made the refugees the most vulnerable set of people. The borders refugees had to cross for safety were abruptly closed to stop the spread of disease. Refugees are in the direst situation ever. They struggle to survive with undetermined nationality, facing increased food and economic insecurity and with no access to health and protection services.

The refugee crisis is complicated to resolve due to many factors. Their return to homeland is not feasible due to the never ending conflict in their home countries, resettlement is difficult due to the inadequate resources to accommodate them in host nations and also due to their national/ legal policies. People who struggle to resettle have issues with documentation, citizenship and also suffer targeted racist attacks. The traumatised people among them should be provided assistance to rebuild their lives safeguarding their dignity and by providing them agency. It is a herculean task but it is the responsibility of every administrative leader, policy maker, human rights organisation to make sure they deserve a normal life. Regardless of nationality, religion, gender, economic or social status each of us should contribute to this as each of us should work with the mission and vision of sharing the spirit of Universal Brotherhood.

Works Cited

Baak, Melanie. "Once a Refugee, Always a Refugee? The haunting of the refugee label in resettlement." *Refugee Journeys.* JSTOR. Web. 2021. https://www.jstor.org/stable/j.ctv1h45md2.7, pp. 51-70.

Ballengee, Jennifer and David Kelman, eds. *Trauma and Literature in an Age of Globalisation.* New York: Routledge, 2021, pp. 141-154.

Herman, Judith. *Trauma and Recovery: The Aftermath of Violence: From Domestic Abuse to Political Terror.* New York: Basic, 2015.

Hirsch, Marianne. *The Generation of Postmemory: Writing and Visual Culture after the Holocaust.* New York: Columbia UP, 2012.

Hosseini, Khaled. *Sea Prayer.* New York: Riverhead Books, 2018.

Alan Kurdi. https://en.wikipedia.org/wiki/Death_of_Alan_Kurdi. Accessed on 4th July 2020.

Khaled Hosseini. www.khaledhosseini.com. Accessed on 10th July 2020.

"Global Reports." www.unhcr.org. Accessed on 2nd August 2020.

"Global Trends." www.unhcr.org. Accessed on 2nd August 2020.

CHAPTER 13

Female Trauma in Margaret Atwood's *Oryx and Crake*

Soumya S. J and Dr. N. U. Lekshmi

Margaret Atwood's 2003 novel *Oryx and Crake* is a speculative fiction with various themes and motifs. A world after a complete destruction created by the over use of science, war and global warming is presented through a post-apocalyptic era. The characters of the novel represent the victimisation of a modern world where there is no consideration towards humanity. The major character Snowman or Jimmy appears in two genres, one is a pre- apocalyptic world and the other is a post-apocalyptic world. In the novel, many of the characters undergo certain traumatic conditions. The title character, Oryx's situation is one of them. Jimmy and his mother faces depression in many occasions which lead to their trauma. Eventually all these characters overcome the situation to certain extent. In the case of Oryx, her entire life is a result of her pathetic and traumatic life experiences. From a highly insecure life she tries to find out solace even though that does not last long.

The introduction of Oryx itself is sympathetic. Jimmy and Crake see Oryx for the first time in a child pornography site. Surprisingly the two boys are only ten and eleven years old. In a pre-apocalyptic period, the moral destruction of young boys are explained here. They see little Oryx in a porn site. She along with two other children are engaging in sexual activities. Atwood gives an explanation to their activities which are really haunting for the readers. The pathetic situation can be seen when Oryx looks at the camera directly. Her childish and sympathetic face explains the trauma she goes through in the forced sex work. As Jimmy is more humane than Crake, he cannot enjoy the video and the eyes of Oryx haunts him as well as the readers from then onwards. Even in the present time itself, Jimmy as Snowman hears the voice of Oryx is an after effect of this haunting. Whenever Snowman sees Oryx's children, he moves to his past and thus to the memories of Oryx.

The back ground of Oryx is revealed through an investigation made by Jimmy. He remembers the tedious effort he undertakes to summarise about Oryx. The fragmented information he has collected about Oryx are not a completed one. Jimmy has a photograph of Oryx for gathering information about her. Even though Jimmy finds Oryx, she responds evasively to his questions. This shows her attitude towards her absurd life. Here Jimmy is compassionate towards her but Crake finds her earlier than Jimmy to use her sexually.

The trauma of Oryx starts from her childhood. The information collected by Jimmy about Oryx is highly pathetic. Oryx's life is a product of poverty. The poverty of Asian countries and their forced sexual labour are revealed here. Oryx is born in a poor village in Asia. Oryx has only a vague memory about her early child hood. In that village most of the families are poor so they sell their children to a business man named Uncle En. This business man is settled in the city and he takes away the children. As per the information given by this man, the children work as flower sellers. Some of the families sell more than one child to him. Thus, Oryx along with two of her brothers are sold to him.

The chaos in Oryx's life starts from there. She along with two of her brothers travel to an unknown city. How much will the little child's fears then be without her parents? How much will be the trauma experienced by her? When they reach the city Uncle En confines them with other children. They also have the same stories like Oryx. A group of children with same traumatic faces. Even though in the beginning they sell flowers, later Oryx's angelic look and fragile nature put her into the danger of sexual predators. In Oryx's memory, one man asked her to come along with him and when she says this to Uncle En, he tells her to go with him. She has no option other than that of going with him. Later, Uncle En regularly takes her to different hotels and makes money out of it. When Oryx remembers all these things for Jimmy, she cannot hide her childhood trauma from her face.

Then onwards, she becomes a child pornographic artist. A video during that period is viewed by Jimmy and Crake. Both of these young men have affinity towards her. When Crake uses her sexually, Jimmy has an intense care for her. Crake and Oryx eventually become life partners and despite all the traumas, she starts a new life with much positive attitude. Crake's attitude towards her is purely materialistic even after their marriage. Still, she finds happiness in various activities. She starts to work as a teacher in Crake's estate. There she can enjoy her teaching profession. While teaching the children of Crake, the artificially created fellows, she overcomes her trauma through the art of teaching.

Jimmy arrives again in her life during this period. There they start a secret affair. They have night rides and many private moments. During this period Oryx has totally overcome her trauma. She starts to enjoy the positive side of life. Jimmy's non-materialistic love helps Oryx to find happiness in her life. Still, she never reveals all of her secrets to Jimmy. In the present time also, Snowman is confused about her character. When Jimmy asks whether Crake is aware about their relation, Oryx gives only a smile. Soon after Crake kills Oryx in front of Jimmy. It becomes clear that Oryx's life with Crake is a pathetic one and she can live a happy life only with Jimmy. Oryx remains a mystery till the end. Snowman also has a confused knowledge about her, whenever he thinks about Oryx. Oryx's life is a mystery mostly because of her bad childhood experiences. Even though she is a sexual toy for others, she has expected a heartfelt love from Jimmy. In the present time, when Snowman remains as the only human survivor, he always wants to hear the voice of Oryx. Her trauma is understood only by Snowman and even though it is an uncompleted story.

Oryx is the feminine representation in the novel *Oryx and Crake*. Apart from all the other incidents in the novel, Oryx stands differently. She grows by her traumatic life in past as well as in the present. Her final images are very much stubborn and the critics call her as extreme masculine. Oryx is the quintessential and oppressed feminine representation in the novel. Even though Jimmy's mother is there, she is in depression for a long period. Oryx tries to re-build her life and tries to get real love till her end. Thus, the novel is about the trauma in different characters on the social binary system- feminine and masculine. Jimmy represents the masculine trauma and Oryx, the feminine trauma. Oryx falls in danger because of her femininity and thus she creates a masculinity within herself to stand strong. This is confusing. A woman can be strong only when she remains masculine inside. On the contrary Jimmy also goes through traumatic situations even though he is a male. So, it is clear that there is no connection with gender variations with reference to depression and trauma.

Snowman remembers Jimmy's adolescent experience with Oryx. "Several years passed. They must have passed, thinks Snowman: he cannot actually remember much about them, did he have zits, was that it? He cannot remember having any; though, as he recalls, the faces of his rivals were covered in them." (59)

Snowman cannot remember all the incidents related to Oryx. He is the only bridge connected with Oryx's life to the readers. From his limited memories he still remembers the trauma she goes through in her life. That is the reason behind his caring for Oryx even in the last stages. Crake marries Oryx by understanding her life as a prostitute. Thus, he maintains an authority upon her rather than an unconditional love. In the case of Jimmy, he loves her as something precious. Jimmy always wants to keep their relationship as a secret and hides as much he can. Oryx is not much concerned about the secrecy of the relation. It is a relief from all the traumas she goes through. So, she never cares about Crake and his understanding about Oryx's relation with Jimmy. It is clear that Oryx's life with Crake is an expansion of her childhood trauma. There she does not have any freedom or individuality.

Oryx and Crake is a futuristic novel. Its major concern is about genetic engineering. Still it deals about human's condition in a genetically modified world, where science and technologies are conquering humanity and the human feelings. Snowman and Oryx are examples of the victims. They are forced to hide their emotions and those supressed emotions comes out as their trauma. In the case of Oryx, she is forced by Crake to be a part of his non-humane genetical modification. That guilt also confuses in her the last stage of life. There she starts an illegal relationship with Jimmy and that makes Crake angry. After Crake has killed Oryx, her trauma transfers to Jimmy once again. He put himself in a container with the genetically modified creatures and also with the corpse of Oryx. The only happiness Jimmy has felt is that, there is no other owner for Oryx's dead body as Crake is also murdered by Jimmy.

Another major woman character in the novel who is under trauma is Jimmy's mother, Sharon. Readers are not aware about the life of Sharon before her marriage. Snowman's emotional memories about his mother is the only way to understand the traumatic life she has undergone. Sharon wants to live a peaceful life with her family. She believes in nature and its beauty. In the case of Jimmy's father, he spends his time in researching about new scientific discoveries and genetically modified creatures. One of that creatures is a rakunk. Even though Jimmy is fond of his pet, Sharon is disturbed due to its confinement. One of the major noticeable things in this matter is, the children are the most affected by this trauma in family. Especially in the case of mothers, the children become alone amidst of many people. Here in the case of Jimmy, he also tries hard to get back his mother as a normal woman. The depression and trauma are unexplainable to anyone. Still little Jimmy tries his best to get her back.

Jimmy and his parents live in a place called Helthwyzer Compound. It is a big area and more luxurious than organic farms. Sharon is not satisfied to live there because she feels there as a prisoner. She starts to express her dissatisfaction through her behaviour and opinion. No one listens to her except little Jimmy. The dissatisfaction grows as depression in her and eventually a kind of trauma arouses in her. Her husband's negligence and his extra marital relation with his colleague are also some reasons behind her depression. Jimmy's father is a busy man who spends most of his time in researching about new genetic modification. One day Jimmy's father comes home to take a break after creating pigoons, the creatures help to grow human skin cells. He wants to celebrate his new genetically modified creatures but Jimmy's mother becomes upset to know about this creation. She refuses to celebrate and criticized her husband for creating this morally reprehensible object. She becomes depressed seeing all these innovations and she fears to lose a beautiful world. Sharon's concern towards Jimmy can be seen in these lines. "Leave Daddy alone, said his mother. Daddy is thinking. That's what they pay him for. He does not have time for you." (113)

Jimmy grows increasingly detached from his parents. His mother's condition becomes worse. Even though he tries to bring back her, his most concern is towards his pet rakunk named Killer. In a strong anxious stage, Jimmy's mother destroys her husband's computer and leaves home along with the rakunk. Jimmy is shocked knowing these things. One of the most emotional situations in novel is described in this section. Jimmy's utmost worry in losing his mother and his pet are shown here. He cries for both of them but he is sadder due to the loss of the rakunk. For the readers' anxiety, Sharon takes this rakunk to release it in the forest. She wants to make it a free animal rather than confining it in the compound. To Jimmy's consolation, he receives a letter from his mother and it is clear that she has left only her married life in order to get some mental peace. For a long period, the where abouts of Sharon is unknown to Jimmy and others. "He loved her so much when he made her unhappy". (41)

Jimmy sees Sharon in a TV show. She is presented as an activist along with other activists. They are protesting against the anti-environmental activities. As Sharon is deeply depressed by the anti-environmental activities, she spends her entire life to protect the world from bio-terrorism. This is how she overcomes her trauma to an extent. Thus, Sharon's escape from trauma is different from Oryx. In the case of Sharon, her concern about her son Jimmy is always there. That is evident in the last word before her death. It is about the rakunk, Killer. It is clearly an information given to Jimmy. So, Sharon, even though she is away from her family, she has concern towards her son and that remains an element of trauma in her.

There are other characters also who undergo trauma in the novel other than Sharon and Oryx. Both of these characters directly or indirectly affect Jimmy also. Mother's disappearance and Oryx's story has affected Jimmy pathetically. He has many different traumatic periods in his life. The first one is after his mother's disappearance with his pet rakunk. He becomes alone when his mother left him and he overcomes his trauma when he meets Crake. His next experience with trauma is connected with Oryx. When he sees Oryx's porn videos and her sympathetic eyes, he again falls in trauma. After many years, an investigation officer shows Jimmy the assassination of his mother, Sharon. It is a heavy shock for him to see his own mother's death. That is his next traumatic experience and he is in trauma for a long time.

Margaret Atwood's novel *Oryx and Crake* is a mixture of many themes and motifs which highlight the thematic changes. The study on *Oryx and Crake* is multi-dimensional as it addresses the characters' trauma, depression, revenge, loneliness and suffering.

Works Cited

Atwood, Margaret. *Oryx and Crake*. McClelland and Stewart, 2003. Print.

Horney, Karen. *Self-Analysis*. Norton, 1939. Print.

Kurtz, Roger. *Trauma and Literature*. Oxford Publication, 2018. Print.

CHAPTER 14

Trauma Narratives and Herstories in K R Meera

Dr. Reji A L

The Greek trauma, or "wound," originally refers to an injury inflicted on a body. But, in Freud's text, the term trauma is understood as a wound inflicted not upon the body but upon the mind. The unknowing acts of the survivor and against his very will – the experience that Freud calls "traumatic neurosis" – emerges as the unwitting re-enactment of an event that one cannot simply leave behind. Literature, like psychoanalysis, is interested in the complex relation between knowing and not knowing. And it is, indeed at the specific point at which knowing and not knowing intersect that the language of literature and the psychoanalytic theory of traumatic experience precisely meet. Trauma narratives, does not simply represent the violence of a collision but also conveys the impact of its very incomprehensibility.

In the introduction of *Unclaimed Experience: Trauma, Narrative and History*, Cathy Caruth says: trauma is a kind of double telling, the oscillation between a crisis of death and the correlative crisis of life: between the story of the unbearable nature of an event and the story of the unbearable nature of its survival.

Dreams occurring in traumatic neuroses have the characteristic of repeatedly bringing the person back into the situation of his accident, a situation from which he wakes up in another fright. What one returns to in the flashback is not the incomprehensibility of one's near death, but the very incomprehensibility of one's own survival.

In its general definition, trauma is described as the response to an unexpected or overwhelming violent event or events that are not fully grasped as they occur, but return later in repeated flashbacks, nightmares, and other repetitive phenomena. The belatedness and incomprehensibility remain at the heart of this repetitive seeing.

Shoshana Felman and Dori Laub's Testimony: Crises of Witnessing in Literature, Psychoanalysis and History was published in 1992, Cathy Caruth's edited collection Trauma: Explorations in Memory in 1995 and her monograph Unclaimed Experience: Trauma, Narrative and History in 1996 are undoubtedly the books which opened up the Humanities to Trauma.

In "Trauma Theory: Contexts, Politics, Ethics" Susannah Radstone offers a critique of trauma theory's model of subjectivity, and its relations with theories of referentiality and representation, history and testimony. The critiques of referentiality derived from structuralism, post-structuralism, psychoanalysis, semiotics and deconstruction suggest that representations bear only a highly mediated or indirect relation to actuality. Trauma theory also moves through and beyond that proposal. For Dori Laub, the absence of traces gives rise to his formulation of the aetiology of trauma as 'an event without a witness' (Testimony: Crises of Witnessing in Literature, Psychoanalysis and History 75-92). Bessel A. Van der Kolk and others have argued in Traumatic Stress: The Effects of Overwhelming Experience on Mind, Body and Society, in the words of Ruth Leys, that 'the traumatic event is encoded in the brain in a different way from ordinary memory' (Trauma: A Genealogy 7).

Alongside an emphasis on memory and brain function, this 'postmodern' psychology includes also a strand that emphasises intersubjectivity and the role of the listener or witness in the bringing to consciousness of previously unassimilated memory.

For Ruth Leys, mimetic and anti-mimetic tendencies cannot be strictly divided from each other. Leys's account of the differences between the anti-mimetic and mimetic paradigms also draws attention to the question of the traumatised subject's relation to the aggressor. Whereas the mimetic paradigm 'posits a moment of identification with the aggressor (...) the antimimetic theory depicts violence as purely and simply an assault from without (TG 299).

> Hypnosis (...) played a major theoretical role in the conceptualisation of trauma (...) because the tendency of hypnotized persons to imitate or repeat whatever they were told to say or do provided a basic model for the traumatic experience. Trauma was defined as a situation of dissociation or 'absence' from the self in which the victim unconsciously imitated or identified with the aggressor or traumatic scene in a situation that was

likened to a state of heightened suggestibility or hypnotic trance. (TG, 8-9)

In Caruth, and in Felman and Laub, it is the unexperienced nature of the event, which give rise to Post-Traumatic Stress Disorder. Trauma distorts the power, common sense, and understanding of the traumatised person. Testimony refers to a relation of witnessing between the subject of trauma and the listener.

Trauma at Home: After 9/11 edited by Judith Greenberg analyses the wide-ranging reflections on understanding, representing, and surviving trauma after the terrorist attacks of September 11. Toni Morrison's *Home* depicts the siblings' traumatic memories of childhood abuse, also drawing into play the wider history of slavery and racist persecution and lynchings, as well as Frank's trauma as a veteran of the Korean war, and his many symptoms of Post-Traumatic Stress Disorder (PTSD).

Human beings are in search of security, order, connection, certainty, meaning, identity, and love. Gender identity is characterised by the public expression of the gender role. K R Meera's novels critique the traditional female identities of 'pativratas' with counter narratives. It also challenges male identity and masculinity which create false hegemonic traits for males. Judith Butler challenges the performative trait of gender and also the relation of gender and identity in her book *Gender Trouble: Feminism and the Subversion of Identity.*

In *The Unseeing Idol of Light,* the narrative unfolds the realms of light and darkness through the philosophical underpinnings. Seeing is used as a metaphor. Prakash could not see the sufferings of others like Rajani.

What is there in a name? Even if it is Deepthi or not, the sufferings, angst and agony suffered by female psyche and body is undefinable and provides a traumatic experience throughout within the narrative space through the different female characters like Jyothi, Deepthi, Rajani, Shalini etc.

Characters' name, especially the central characters – Prakash, Deepthi, Jyothi, Sooraj – are synonymous with light, though some of them are struggling for sight. Trauma causes temporary or ongoing mental and physical health concerns in different individuals. Prakash lost his eyesight after the missing of his wife Deepthi. He suffers from trauma. The shocking, painful and distressing experience of trauma here results in temporary or gradual losing of his eyesight. Sooraj is a blind orphan supposed to be the first-born child of Prakash and Deepthi. Jyothi, another version of Deepthi, lost her husband in a train journey. She was gang raped and left in the platform. She lost her new born baby as a result of the atrocities done to her body by a group of eighteen men. After hearing her story, Rajani asked why she didn't return to her husband. Jyothi retorts: "No woman who had accepted the sweat, saliva and semen of eighteen men in one night would be able to return to her first man... " (209).

In search of Deepthi both Prakash and Syam had to visit police stations, mortuaries and railway tracks several times. Some psychiatrists, such as Worden, argue that viewing the body helps to bring home the reality of loss, and that viewing helps in the grieving process, because bonds with the deceased need to be severed so that the survivor can make new attachments. Prakash wanted Shyam to identify the body. Identifying an unknown body in a mortuary makes a feeling of vomiting for Prakash's friend Shyam. They couldn't identify the body of Deepthi anywhere.

Meena Kandasamy says: *The Unseeing Idol of Light* is engrossing forensic, rich in complexity and intense in its sadness. K R Meera's prose is always a pleasure, a place where language becomes landscape. It is a haunting tale that explores love and loss, blindness and sight, obsession and suffering and the poignant interconnections between them.

The "black hole of desolation created by Deepti's departure" (4) glued on Prakash's face. The images used in the text are very powerful. "A thousand-odd bats, hanging upside down and frantically beating their wings" (4). Prakash's life too is hung upside down like a bat. The sky appeared swollen with rain clouds and the moss - infested roof of the next building gleamed demonically (6). The appearance of the woman in the shelter who suffered from dementia, was pathetic. She seemed devoid of life, unmoving, wearing a dress twice her size, exposing bones that jutted out of her emaciated frame. She did not look up. She is called by the inmates as Lily, but later identified by someone after viewing the newspaper advertisement as Suprabha.

The image of the suicide of his father haunted Prakash. Ravi, his father hanged himself from the huge mango tree beyond the canal. Prakash had been eight when his father died. At a glance, his father's body, covered his head with judge's rob, hands uplifted, legs drawn apart resembled "a gigantic bat". It appears recurrently in Prakash's nightmares. After the death of his father, his Amma lost sleep and had a feeling that "someone is calling out from the gates... Someone!" (30) When the loved ones vanish, the nights of those who are left behind become choked with a dark emptiness.

Food is an effective trigger of deeper memories of feelings and emotions, internal states of the mind and body. 'Mambazhapulissery' brings home some painful memories for Prakash. The lone hint that Prakash's Acchan had given was his insistence on having 'Mambazhapulissery' for his last supper. Deepthi had conceived in September. Much before the news was confirmed, Deepti had dreamt of feeding rice balls with 'Mambazhapulissery' to a little boy. During her pregnancy, she yearned for 'Mambazhapulissery'.

Prakash refused to purchase a TV in his home for a very long time, because before Deepti had gone missing, they had talked about TV and Deepti's laughter still resonates in Prakash's ears. So for Prakash, TV is associated with misfortune.

Rajani worked in a Blind School. When Shyam and Prakash entered the Blind School, they noticed one boy whose eyes were devoid of irises. The white emptiness, staring out from that winsome face was frightening for Shyam.

Self-injury is a harmful way to cope with emotional pain, intense anger and frustration. Rajani had the experience of sixteen suicide attempts in her twenty-three years. She had sentenced her body. When Deepti is compared to a blazing lamp, Rajani is compared to a gloomy hurricane lamp. She had a bad childhood. Her Amma suffered a lot from her cruel father. She is compared to a butterfly that had metamorphosed back into a worm after losing its wings. Due to his sexual passion, when her father undressed and got naked in front of little Rajani, her mother threw kerosene over his body and lit a matchstick and set him on fire. Amma had hanged herself. After that she lived in the homes of different relatives. All those years, she continued her attempts to make better knots. But every time "her head slipped right through the noose like a greasy frog that eluded a catcher's grip" (40).

The narrative is caught in between past and present and progresses to future pages. Prakash tries to find Deepti in Rajani. But when he comes back to present day reality, he is haunted by the memories of Deepti. Prakash gratifies his strong desire in Rajani. At last deserted by everyone, she hanged herself after giving birth to a baby girl. She is the epitome of the exploitation and suffering and afflicted pain from the male world.

The Angel's Beauty Spots is a collection of three novellas. Angela was killed in front of her children. Her husband was the killer. "He thrust the knife deep into her fair-skinned, well-rounded belly again and again.... The chilling scent of blood filled the room. Like brooding storm clouds, fear filled the room with darkness and cold."

The popular Victorian image of the ideal wife/woman was 'the Angel in the House'. The Angel was passive and powerless, meek, charming, graceful, sympathetic, self-sacrificing, pious, and above all--pure. The phrase 'Angel in the House' comes from the title of an immensely popular poem by Coventry Patmore, in which he holds his angel-wife up as a model for all women.

Angela was expected to be an 'Angel', devoted and submissive to her husband, though he was aggressive, cruel and forced her to be a woman of the street. Virginia Woolf, wrote in 1931, "killing the Angel in the House was part of the occupation of a woman writer." Taking these words to heart, in *The Angel's Beauty Spots,* K R Meera, as a writer, freed Angela from "the angel of the house" to a woman in search of love in others' door steps because she was more sinned against than sinning. It is a critique of the male dominant discourses and the creation of home as a holy space where he used to carry the idol of woman as a goddess. K R Meera's writing is powerful and frequently questions the traditional concept of 'man must be pleased'.

Angela once told Narendran: "This body is a huge liability. Very hard to lug *without* a job! And hard to find a job *with* it!" (12) Angela smiled when her husband Alex stabbed her. It did not hurt, because he had killed her long time ago. That day, Alex's friend swooped down on her and "played with her lifeless body like a cat slowly killing a mouse" (20). That was the day Angela had died.

"Mummy never cried" (21), Ann remembers her smiling face. She turned tears into laughter. One day or the other several men came and walked off in her life as the owner of the jewellery shop forced her to satisfy his lust in front of her children. She slapped him hard with her soiled hand and shouted at him to leave.

Angela admits once: "I know it is a sin to sell my body. But I don't sell my body, I sell empathy. I have only pity for him.... He knows that he'll receive love only for his money" (23). Her two children were separated. Ann was sent with Alex's sister. Narendran was going to send Irene, his own blood, to a poor home.

In "And Forgetting the Tree, I... ", ten-year-old Radhika, forgotten by her father on the road side, was raped by a woodcutter. That memory strikes Radhika "like a thunderbolt and hurls her to the floor. It pierces right through her brain cells, smashes them up... " (33-34). When the father and the daughter saw each other in the police station, she was naked, "the clotted blood clung to her small bony thighs, like dried, blackened moss staining the bark of a tree." She was raped again by Christy in the hotel room. When Ajith her husband said, on their very first night, that he had married her only and only because he had felt sorry for her, the soil under her feet came loose.

When Christy returned to her life one day, lightning tore through Radhika's brain. Her mind splintered. She lost track of time and space. "Their relationship was like a tree struck by lightning. He had sunk his roots deep into her.... its core turned into ashes, its roots stopped feeding on moisture, leaves stopped eating light, naturally the tree fell.... like an unidentified corpse... " (37).

The memory of her past came back again to Radhika. "Acchan. The town. Waiting. The shed. The bar named Peruvazhiyambalam. The pathos of a girl forgotten by her father" (41). Radhika shows a tendency to relive the past and to exist in the present as if she was still fully in the past, with no distance from it. She forgot all the points she had noted for a case. Finally, she lost it.

Radhika dreamt of the woodcutter one night. In the dream, she was pregnant. He tied her up on the cot with a strong rope. He raised the axe and brought it down on her swollen belly. She woke up screaming. This can be treated as a moment of PTSD.

When Radhika described the mishap with each and every minute details to Christy after ten years, she suffered that day all over again. She repeatedly acting out – the tendency to repeat something compulsively – the agony due to trauma. After that incident, her Acchan became neurotic, showing symptoms of madness. He wept, "Parvathy, my Parvathy." They are compelled to take him to Painkulam for shock therapy (49).

Radhika remembered her first meeting with Christy. Lonacchan and Thankamma made her to sell her body for money. When she struggled to escape, he pushed her down on the floor and raped her. He consumes her body many times after that. All these memories came flooding back. From Christy's brothers, she happened to know that Christy had been taken to Painkulam regularly for shock treatment. They said that it was a hereditary disease and could not be cured. The place called Painkulam had always made Radhika very uneasy and nervous. The headaches that had once troubled her had returned. She closed the door, bolted the windows, darkened the bed room and lay down (60). Once, when she started reading Christy's book, the letters inside gave her a burning sensation. Darkness rushed into her eyes. Her consciousness dimmed. She flung the books away, slammed her head against the wall, the skin on her forehead split open (66).

Christy's true self came out, when he came to know that his child was in Radhika's womb. He slapped and threatened to kill her. Then he appeared with a trick to ruin the child. He made her believe that they are going to be married in Kaipamangalam church. He pulled out a minnu and tied it around her neck. When they reached the graveyard, he turned brutal, beat her mercilessly, pushed her down, and drove his knee hard into her lower belly. After killing the child, he plucked the minnu from her neck (71).

The image of a tree is employed throughout the narrative: 'The raw scent of wood chopped by the woodcutter' (33); Radhika's 'huge memory tree'; and Ajith's love like 'paring off branch after branch and finally cutting the trunk'; Christy's love is 'a strange tree which sprouts from fallen leaves, fallen branches, fallen fruit; the outer shell may dry up, the core lives'; at last Radhika feels 'love is a strange thorn, a poisonous thorn, terrible pain when it pierces and is pulled out' (79) and 'the doctor plucked Aristotle Christy out with the forceps, leaf by leaf, shoot by shoot' (85-86).

In "The Deepest Blue", the narrator warns the readers that chaste wives (in the 'satisavitri' mould) and monogamous men (in the 'maryaadaapurushottam' mould) are advised against reading this account (101). The writer is expressing her defiance and rebellious attitude against the ways she is expected to follow.

The question of who and what is considered real and true is apparently a question of knowledge. For Foucault, Knowledge is Power. Knowledge and Power are not separable. One of the first tasks of a radical critique is to discern the relation "between mechanisms of coercion and elements of knowledge" (50). K R Meera in "The Deepest Blue" disrupts the settled knowledge of family, wife, love and sex. She created a world of fantasy which pushes the boundaries of the real and questions the contemporary notions of reality. These practices of new modes of realities take place through embodiment where the body exceeds and reworks the norm.

The story's movement is like a serpent's movement upon a rock. The narrator 'I' describes her love "a languid serpent, an utterly venomous one" (103). Snakes appear in a number of different religions, taking on the roles of good and evil depending on the circumstances. Snake is used in the Bible as an instrument of Satan, sent to tempt Eve and encourage her to disobey God. These scaly creatures have evoked fear and awe in readers. Snakes often represent fertility in myth and literature.

"The unmarried have keener eyesight. Once you're married, it diminishes" (108). The narrator reminds that her husband wrote four or five whole essays about a small birthmark before marriage. But all stopped at once when the 'thali' tied around her neck as a noose. She felt uneasiness within the four walls of the house like "a snake stifled in a wicker basket" (108). She has bitten the hermit in the serpent grove and he turned blue completely. Gender norms are reproduced here by bodily practices. The narrator keeps on saying love is not only strange, but also painful. She revives the physicality and sensuousness of love through the performance of her body and defeats the hypocritical spirituality of love. As Butler pointed out gender is constructed through acts and traits and is exhibited by the body which is used as a weapon to reconstruct the gendered identities here.

Colours are symbolic of many inexpressible things and are widely used as recurrent motifs in the novels of K R Meera. The colour blue is used in the narrative as an icon of love, pain, loss and desire. It suggests free and liberated ideas, breaking away from the regular expected way of life. In this narrative the woman defeats the man, makes him a slave. She becomes his owner as against the traditional male superiority theory. She calls it "an honest burning silver of experience" (102) and compares her love to "the house freshly on fire" (129). K R Meera questions recurrently the structuralities of the familial discourses and breaks it in the space of an old 'nalukettu' which was tightly closed once, where lies the past memories of silenced female voices and utter darkness. She makes it open as the light peeps in and the fresh air dances and gives 'the haunted spirits' salvation.

Tulsi in *The Poison of Love* mirrored lives and plight of many women. This world has produced devastated countless Tulsis. "My love was like a serpent that had swallowed its own tail. It twisted around in circles, trying to consume itself" (29). The travel and transformation from Tulsi to Meera sadhu was long and severe. It was an ordeal. Madhav loved Tulsi like a joke. But she realised it too late after being the mother of two children. She was one among her twenty seven lovers. Vengeance started inflaming her mind. "Madhav's love was an acid that corroded the vessel itself, her flesh burned, bones melted" (45). "Love was like the demoness Putana" (81). She gave poisonous milk to her children. Tulsi whispers: "we have to defeat your father... leave him before he can abandon us" (91).

The dissociation of unassimilated memories and a focus on the traumatic nature of unconscious associations frequently appeared in K R Meera's narratives. The complex configuration of love, hatred, and loss are intertwined. Meera weaves history, romance and the politics of the present into a narrative of incredible complexity. Each story invokes the inner violence of contemporary society in Kerala. Meera reveals how trauma as a catastrophe, either individual or collective, affects shockingly male and female characters' identities, so that their physical and psychological responses can be analysed in terms of diagnosis of the trauma and its aftermath.

Works Cited

Butler, Judith. *Gender Trouble: Feminism and the Subversion of Identity*. New York: Routledge, 1999.

Caruth, Cathy. ed., *Trauma: Explorations in Memory*. Johns Hopkins University Press, 1995.

.... *Unclaimed Experience: Trauma, Narrative and History*. Johns Hopkins University Press, 1996.

Foucault, Michel. "What is Critique?" in *The Politics of Truth*, eds. Sylvère Lotringer and Lysa Hochroth, Semiotext(e), 1997.

Felman, Shoshana, et al. *Testimony: Crises of Witnessing in Literature, Psychoanalysis, and History*. United Kingdom, Routledge, 1991.

Greenberg, Judith. ed., *Trauma at Home*. Nebraska University Press, 2003.

Laub, Dory. *Testimony: Crises of Witnessing in Literature, Psychoanalysis and History*. Routledge, 1992.

Leys, Ruth. *Trauma: A Genealogy*. University of Chicago Press, 2000.

Meera, K. R. *The Angel's Beauty Spots.* Translated by J. Devika. Aleph, 2019.

.... *The Unseeing Idol of Light.* Translated by Ministhy S. Penguin, 2018.

.... *The Poison of Love.* Translated by Ministhy S. Penguin, 2017.

Radstone, Susannah. "Trauma theory: Contexts, Politics, Ethics." University of East London Institutional Repository, 2007.

Worden J. W. *Grief Counselling and Grief Therapy: A Handbook for the Mental Health Practitioner.* 2nd ed. Routledge, 1991.Google Scholar.

CHAPTER 15

Abominated and Alienated: The Trauma of the Immigrants in Paolo Bachigalupi's *The Drowned Cities*

Sajena A. and Dr. Sheeba S Nair

Paolo Bachigalupi's *The Drowned Cities,* a future based novel, set in America is an adult fiction which pinpoints the struggles faced by the young migrants and how they escape the war-torn drowned cities. It also exposes the dark side of the corporates, the predicaments of the immigrants in the drowned cities and the effects of the rising sea level which lead to the destruction of the human kind. The main cities in America are submerged in sea water due to the rising sea level and completely ravaged by the climate change, social and economic ruin. People lose their shelter and become refugees in their own land. Two groups named, Union Patriotic Force (UPF) and the Army of God are rivals and they fight to inhabit the half-submerged cities. The corporates have created bioengineered half-human and half-animal called augment with high intelligence and extreme physical power. It escapes from the clutches of his master and roam around the drowned cities.

Trauma is not a disorder but a reaction to a kind of wound caused by actual life events and harmful situations which may happen once or repeatedly. It is caused by expressions of violence, such as sexual abuse, racism, discrimination, and can be complex. Traumatic events involve the confrontation with the war, accident, serious illness, disaster, violence and so on. Bessel Van pens, traumatic events such as family and social violence, rapes and assaults, disasters, wars, accidents and predatory violence confront people with such horror and threat that it may temporarily or permanently alter their capacity to cope, their biological threat perception and their concept of themselves". (7)

Trauma theory in literary studies captured attention with the publication of Cathy Caruth's *Unclaimed Experience: Trauma, Narrative, and History*. Merriam Webster defines Trauma as, "a disordered psychic or behavioural state resulting from severe mental or emotional stress or physical injury". It affects severely an individual's self-perception and the insights regarding the external world. Trauma Theory, explores the impact of trauma in an individual or society by analysing the social and psychological aspects.

When an individual confronts or witnesses viciousness in any form like, war, accident or disaster, it may result in a sense of displacement and develops post-traumatic stress disorder in them. It also includes intrusive memories, anxiety, nostalgia, resilience and so on. There is a constant fear in the victims' mind that the traumatic events may occur again. Mahlia, one of the leading characters in *The Drowned Cities*, is a Chinese cast off who along with her friend Mouse struggles to live in the swamps. Mahlia's right arm is cut by the soldiers of the Army of God. Doctor Mahfouz rescues her from the clutches of the soldiers and appoints her as his assistant. Mahlia is introduced in *The Drowned Cities* as, "An orphan girl like Mahlia, who had shown up in Banyan Town with a chopped-off right hand, bleeding dying for help. No one wanted a war maggot in their midst" (36). Mahlia is a young girl, who assists Doctor Mahfouz to treat the people in the village and her desire is to move to Sea Boston, an industrial area and live a peaceful life free from war and destruction.

Xenophobia is an excessive fear or hatred for people of other caste, religion or foreigners. People in the Banyan Town hate Mahlia and constantly blames her for all mishappenings. For instance, when Tani, a young girl dies during her delivery, her father blames Mahlia for the mishap. Mr Salvatore, Tani's father says, "Castoffs like her are bad luck. We should have run her off when we had the chance" (28). He also refers to the Doctor as a fool for appointing a refugee as his assistance. He incessantly calls her "bad luck and death" (26). He also adds that she is born to kill things and it is she who attracts bad luck to the village. He says, "she kills things...everywhere she goes nothing but blood and death" (27). When Mahlia takes Tani's child to Amaya, she too blames Mahlia for the death of Tani and yells at her as, "she didn't need a useless crippled China girl for a nurse...you got the blood right there on your face. China castoff, through and through" (37). Amaya shows her extreme hatred towards Mahlia by saying that she is neither wanted by the Chinese nor by the village people. Likewise, when Alejandro's goats are attacked by the coyotes, they blame Mahlia for casting her eyes over them.

Bachigalupi uses Doctor Mahfouz as his mouthpiece to insist on the view that refugees are also human beings who deserve to live a normal life alike other human beings. He saves Mahlia and Mouse from the soldiers and despite of his financial position he cares for them and also promises Mr. Salvatore that until Tani's child grows up, he will take care of it. When Amaya yells at Mahlia, he advises Mahlia to search for extra food for Amaya and the new born. He often advises Mahlia, "a harmless war orphan is something they may not love, but still, they can empathize. But if you seem violent, they'll see you the same way they see coywolv" (39). Doctor Mahfouz is the only person in the Banyan Town to voice for Mahlia. Mahlia says, "Everyone wanted to be good. They just sometimes needed help finding their way to it…the drowned cities were busy tearing themselves apart once again, but here the doctor was, still talking about how people wanted to be kind and good" (28).

When the Union Patriotic Force (UPF) soldiers happen to see Mahlia in the swamps, they torture her by twisting her arms and incessantly refer to her as "castoff" (87). One of the soldiers calls her as peacemaker and says, "what's a peacekeeper girl doing way out here? This town protecting you?" (87). Another soldier ridicules her appearance and threatens her by pushing the blade inside her mouth. He says, "didn't know there were collaborators hiding out here…thought we cleaned you all out" (88). They make her shout the slogans used by the peacemakers.

The peacemakers are Chinese people who arrived in America and tried to civilise the drowned cities. Nearly fifteen years they colonised in the drowned cities and attempted to reduce the violence by asking people to stop fighting and start farming. They built hospitals for the war victims and medicines with the wordings, "with wishes for peace and well-being from the people of Beijing" (29). Mahlia says, "when the sea level rose, they built huge dikes to protect their coastlines, and floated their greatest cities on the waves, like they did with Island Shanghai" (61). The Chinese are advanced in their thinking and they protected their country by building sea walls. They insisted the people of drowned cities to cease fighting but their attempt to civilise the people ended in vain.

The soldiers ask her to repeat the phrases like, "disarm to farm", "beat your swords into plowshares", "only animals tear each other apart" (111) which are used by the peacemakers at the time of war. Soa, one of the soldiers, scoops a handful of blood from the floor and scours all over her face. She thinks, "first there would be screaming and then there would be blood and then at the end, if she was lucky, she would be dead" (87). Another soldier tries to choke her and Doctor Mahfouz arrives there and saves her from them. When they come to know that she is able to treat wounds they plan to take her as a nurse to care for Ocho, a wounded soldier. When Mahlia plots against the soldiers and escapes to the jungle, the soldiers attack the Banyan Town and the people curse Mahlia and gives a sweeping statement that refugees lack loyalty.

Nostalgia is a psychopathological condition, which occurs in a person, when he or she is alienated or frustrated. Mahlia often feels nostalgic. Tani's corpse reminds her of the brutal murders performed by the soldiers. She thinks, "Tani's death was just a bad luck. Not like most of the deaths she'd seen, where someone died because a soldier boy didn't like the way you talked, or wanted something you had, or didn't like the shape of your eyes" (30). Whenever she faces quandaries in her life, she is nostalgic about her life as a Chinese girl in the Drowned Cities. She thinks about the days when Chinese people donates clothes and rehydration packets to the war victims. When the soldiers constantly addressed her as a Chinese cast off, by referring to the blood on her face, she was reminded of her father's words that she lacked culture and acted like an animal.

Also, when Mouse advises her not to react when people treat her badly, the memories of those horror days and the sufferings occupy her mind. All the other castoffs like her were dead and gone. "The kids who went to the peacekeeper schools, all those almond-eyed kids…Amy Ma and Louis Hsu and Ping Li and all those others…they'd been too civilised to know what to do when the hammer came down" (66). Mouse too shares his story to Mahlia about his sufferings. He says that the soldiers shot his parents and Simon, his brother aypynd burn the farm. They recruited Shane, his elder brother and their attempt to kill him ends futile. He says, "all those bullets they shot at me, and I didn't take a single one, like the Fates put a hand down between me and them" (68) and also adds that he is able to survive because he didn't protest. Likewise, Tool, a half-human and half-animal escapes Sea Boston and get sheltered in the Drowned Cities. He remembers the days when he used to slaughter the refugees and the refugees run before him like a river in the flood. He along with his crew have slaughtered thousands of refugees and hyena-men and consumed their hearts. The intrusive memories of their past often flash in the memory of the characters and interrupt their present events.

Emotional dysregulations are one of the consequences of the traumatic experiences. Some trauma survivors have difficulty regulating emotions such as anger, anxiety, sadness, shame and so on. Cathy Caruth says, "trauma is not locatable in the simple violent or original event in an individual's past, but rather in the way that its very unassimilated nature… returns to haunt the survivor later on." (Caruth 25). Mahlia bursts out to Amaya, when she calls her cast off. She roars, "Maybe I cut you the way the Army of God cut me. See how you do with just a lucky left. How'd you like that?" (38). Also, she confronts Soa, when he constantly calls her a castoff. She says, "I ain't Chinese. I'm Drowned Cities" (89). She also yells at Mr. Salvatore when he says that she put the Fates Eye on Alejandro's goats. She replies, "I'm looking at you, that mean you're dead, too?" (27). In addition to this, she tries to help Tool, despite of the Doctor's warning. Her intention is to escape the Drowned Cities and so she decides to accompany Tool. When the Doctor advises her not to indulge in violence, she says that she "doesn't need someone who talked peace; she needed something that made war" (149). She hesitates to follow the Doctor and stays determined in her decision. She behaves like a mad cat when she is downgraded and treated as an alien by the people.

Resilience is a dynamic process in which the circumstance or the people around an individual influences him or her to come out of the distressing reminiscences. Maintaining a healthy relationship with them and providing a safety environment aid in quick retrieval of their mental health. Experts are of the opinion that resilience must be treated with caution as there are risks involved. Mahlia wanted to escape her past and her desire is to reach Sea Boston and live a life free from oppression. In order to escape from the drowned cities, she forsakes Doctor Mahfouz's advice and accompanies Tool. But Mouse hesitates to follow her and runs with Mahfouz. She even goes to the extent of murdering Amaya, when she runs towards the village to inform about Mahlia and Tool. The Doctor is taken aback when she shouts, "she's going back to the soldiers! If she rats us, we're all dead. Once they got our scent and direction, there's no way we shake free…get her, don't let Amaya get back town" (181). She is also determined in her decision that she is not going to return to the village. She tries to convince the Doctor to accompany her to Boston. Mahlia is aware of the fact that, if she returns to the village, she will be slaughtered by the soldiers. The doctor is shocked to see Mahlia, who has taken the path of violence when she justifies that what she did to the soldiers is right and says, "if I had some guns, I would have killed them" (183).

Existence is one of the maxims of the traumatised people. Mahlia, Tool and Mouse strive to escape war and devastation. Mahlia wants to escape the drowned cities and wish to live a peaceful life. In order to survive, she even ditches the Doctor. She attacks the UPF soldiers like a wounded cat and escapes from there. As the result of her incoherent strategy, the Banyan Town is attacked brutally by the soldiers. The one and only desire she holds in her mind is to survive.

Mahlia and her mother's agony begins once the peacemakers leave the Drowned Cities. Her mother is killed and Mahlia loses her right arm and becomes a castoff. Life as a castoff is tough for Mahlia and Mouse. They both functioned like a "tight little unit" (186). They survive by consuming ant eggs and crawdads. When the army attacks the village, they play dead. Her ordeals are portrayed by Bachigalupi as, "she was always running. Like a rabbit chased by coywolv. Always hunting for some new safe bolt hole, and every time, the soldier boys found her, and forced her to rabbit again" (147). She is completely against the Doctor's insight to stay in the Drowned cities. According to her, there is no place to hide and in drowned cities no one can expect to be safe from the soldiers and the coywolves.

On the other hand, Mouse decides to go to the village along with the Doctor. The soldiers kill the Doctor and recruits Mouse. They name him Ghost and makes him torture the villagers. He sobs when he happens to thrash Aunt Selima and apologies to Donato, an old man for kicking him in the ribs. He often thinks of escaping from the clutches of the soldiers. He says, "I don't want to be a war boy. I'm a coward. I should stand up and fight them or run away, or something" (257).

Meanwhile, Mahlia manipulates the child soldiers and by selling scavenges, gets some money and a shot gun. She threatens an old man and asks him to help her to sail to Sea Boston. He says, "they won't take your kind" (305) and threatens her that if he gets a chance, he may kill her. She says, "I'm dead already, old man. Don't you get it? You kill me, it don't matter. I'm just another castoff. People won't even blink about it, will they? They'd mourn a nailshed girl more than they'd mourn me" (306). These words of Mahlia portray the emotional discomfort endured by her as a refugee. The boat man asks her to hide her face using a cap so that they can easily escape the drowned cities. He says, "a castoff had no chance going in to the drowned cities" (316).

On seeing Mouse, Ocho is reminded of his journey as a soldier. He says to the other soldiers, "my family were fishers. We all got blown in on a hurricane, couldn't paddle out. UPF scooped us up…they thought my eyes looked like the Colonel's so they recruited me" (324). In order to survive, to escape hunger and death, most of the child soldiers in the drowned cities live the life of soldiers. Throughout *The Drowned Cities*, Mahlia, is tormented both mentally and physically. When the soldiers happen to see her in the city, they cut her pinky finger and stabs her. She is tormented both mentally and physically. Finally, rescued by Tool and escapes to Sea Boston. Though the novel ends with a ray of hope, it is unclear whether she will be accepted by the people of Boston.

As an immigrant, Mahlia happens to lose her family, her livelihood and roams as a crippled young woman in the drowned cities. She is unwelcomed by the village people and the soldiers treat her as a trash. Her instinct to escape from the misery attracts more inconveniences to her. She is forced to witness the murder of her loved ones. With a heart full of hope and unbearable pain, she heads towards Boston.

The Drowned Cities, is set in a harsh, brutal futuristic world where everyone is trying to survive. Adi Roberston is of the opinion that *The Drowned Cities* stands out as one of the most brutal pieces of YA fiction. In *The Drowned Cities*, a future Washington DC, was devastated first by flooding and then by endemic violence, where nobody used high technology. Though filled with horror and violence, it ends with a ray of hope. Mahlia climbs the clipper and heads towards Boston with Tool. Thus the painful experiences of the immigrants especially, the mental trauma undergone by the characters is painted artistically by Bachigalupi in *The Drowned Cities.*

Works Cited

Kolk, Bessel Van Der. *Posttraumatic Stress Disorder and the Nature of Trauma.* State of the Art, 2000.

"trauma". Merriam Webster.com, Merriam Webster, 2020. https://www.merriam-webster.com/dictionary/trauma Accessed 21 July 2021.

Bachigalupi, Paolo. *The Drowned Cities.* United States: Little Brown and Company, 2012. Print.

Robertson, Adi. (2012) "They make us this way: Paolo Bachigalupi's 'The Drowned Cities' The Author Return to the Ecological Apocalypse", April 27, 2012.

CHAPTER 16

Imposed Reticence: A Delve into J. M. Coetzee's *Disgrace*

Sreelatha.R.H

South African Literature is the mirror that reflects the life and culture of South Africa. One of the first South African literary works in English Literature is Olive Shreiner's 1883 work *The Story of an African Farm.* The most famous South African work in English Literature is *Cry, the Beloved Country* by Alan Paton which clearly depicts the typical racial fists well with American perceptions of South African society. Paton also produced *Too Late the Phalarope,* another text criticising the Apartheid politics. Another important writer is Nadine Gordimer. Her most famous novel *July's People* depicts the collapse of white minority rule. John Maxwell Coetzee became internationally recognised in 1983 with his Booker Prize winning novel *Life and Times of Michael K.* His novel *Disgrace* won him his second Booker Prize as well as 2000 Commonwealth Writers' Prize. South African English writing has produced two Nobel Prize winners: Nadine Gordimer and J. M. Coetzee.

Trauma is a psychic strike against the normal psychological imperatives or the functioning of the psychological apparatus. Trauma may pave way to interrupted identities. It can be caused by a negative event that causes a long lasting impact on the victims' mental and emotional stability. "Trauma, definition, is unbearable and intolerable" (*The Body Keeps the Score* Prologue). Some common causes of trauma include, rape. As a concept trauma has attracted a great deal of interest in the literary studies. In literature, trauma studies developed in the 1990s. Psychoanalytic theories regarding the origins and effects of trauma rose in the nineteenth century. Consequently, Cathy Caruth is considered to be the pioneer of trauma theory. The impelled silence in some people can be the impact of a traumatic experience undergone by them.

> Contemporary literary trauma theory claims that trauma creates a speechless fright that divides or destroys the identity of the traumatised.

When some people become violent and mentally ill due to the adverse effects of trauma, some goes silent and numbed forever. Judith Lewis Herman opines that, "The conflict between the will to deny horrible events and the will to proclaim them aloud is the central dialect of psychological trauma" (*Trauma and Recovery* Introduction). Silence is something that lies in the space between violence and trauma and it can be consideredto be the most dangerous situation. Silence intensifies the impact of trauma and the cries that go unheard and unwitnessed can bring more terror to one's self and also to others. When people start to hide their own self, no one could hear the silent cries nagging inside. Silence sometimes becomes the voice of rebellion for those who never had the oomph to rebel against their terrors. Bessel A. vander Kolk says that,

> Traumatised people chronically feel unsafe inside their bodies: The past is alive in the form of gnawing interior discomfort. Their bodies are constantly bombarded by visceral warning signs, and, in an attempt to control these processes, they often become expert at ignoring their gut feelings and in numbing awareness of what is played out inside. They learn to hide from their selves. (*The Body Keeps the Score* 97)

In *Disgrace,* the people who take the role of the central figures are the one who has been victimized. *Disgrace* narrates the story of the two silenced female victims of sexual assault. David Lurie is a South African Professor of English who is obsessed with sex. He is attached to a sex worker, Soraya and attempts to have a romantic relationship with her. But Soraya disappears from Lurie's life. Lurie becomes attracted to one of her vulnerable students Melanie Isaacs and rapes her. She struggles a lot to escape herself from the clutches of Lurie but in vain. "She will not know how to deal with him; he ought to let her go. But he is in the grip of something" (18). Melanie becomes numb as ice after the sex series happened to her. She starts bunking classes. Her rejection for Lurie can be clearly seen through her attempts to avoid him but Lurie pursues her and unleashes her from her safe zone.

The novel *Disgrace* is narrated from the perspective of Lurie and the two female characters Melanie and Lucy is silenced forever after the rape. In the beginning of the novel, when Lurie teaches his students and tries to interact with them he always receive a deep silence from them. This symbolically represents the suppressed feelings of Melanie. "Did anyone look it up in a dictionary? Silence What was the living thought? Silence again" (21). The sexual relationship of Lurie and Melanie can never be considered as a romantic one. It is a sheer sexual appetite of Lurie and he thrusts it upon Melanie without any hesitation. Lurie dashed into Melanie's life and made her taste what pain is and what terror of life is. Melanie on the other hand was not resistant but benumbed by the bloody thirst of Lurie.

> He has given her no warning; she is too surprised to resist the intruder who thrusts himself upon her. When he takes her in his arms, her limbs crumble like a marionette's. Words heavy as cluns thud into the delicate of her ear. 'No, not now!' she syas, struggling. 'My cousin will be back!'
>
> But nothing will stop him (20-21)

Lurie continues to pursue Melanie to quench his sexual thirst. Melanie could not stop him, in fact nothing could stop him. Melanie is too weak to resist him and she is too weak to even pour out her emotions. She feels as if she is a little rabbit fettered in the clutches of a fox. The only thing is to avert herself and to bury herself at that moment. Melanie begins to bury herself alive in the terror of the undesired desires. "All she does is avert herself: avert her lips, avert her eyes Not rape, not quite that, but undesired nevertheless, undesired to the corelike a rabbit when the jaws of the fox close on its neck" (25). Lurie gets charged by the offence of raping his student but never admit it and refuses to apologise. He gets fired from the University and goes to his daughter Lucy, who lives in Eastern Cape only to see his daughter in the same situation as Melanie's.

Lucy runs a farm in Eastern Cape with the help of Petrus, a South African. Lurie starts to live with Lucy and helps her in her farming. Lucy living in a South African village, making the native her assistant shows the white supremacy and Lurie fears that the natives may attack her. But Lucy believes Petrus more and he seems to be a good- hearted fellow. There are traces in the novel that Lucy is a lesbian and Helen her partner is out of town now. As Lurie fears, Lucy gets raped by three Coloured people and they turn out to be Petrus' relatives. Lurie again and again asks Lucy to file a case against them for raping her. But she hides the fact that she has been tormented by the three.

> They will read that they are being sought for robbery and assault and nothing else. It will dawn on them that over the body of the woman,

> silence is being drawn like a blanket. *Too ashamed, they will say to each other, too ashamed to tell,* and they will chuckle luxuriously, recollecting their exploit. (110)

Lucy falls silent day by day and now Lurie could understand the reason behind Melanie's reticence. The women who should strive against the injustice done to them are now silenced because of the interrupted mind. The ascribed meaning of the world around them and their life is now shattered by the bloody hands of male chauvinism. Melanie and Lucy avoid attending the trial because trauma has interrupted their healthy mental state and linguistic mapping. They cannot prove the society what happened to them through their words because trials are just how well people explain, what they have gone through. "trials are not about principles; they are about how well you put yourself across" (188). Melanie and Lucy succumb themselves to the fate and submit themselves to the trauma that interrupted their normalcy. They now accept trauma as their new normalcy through the imposed reticence. Lucy and Melanie withdraw themselves to the world of suppression and silence because they cannot express their unheard wailing.

People who express their mishaps suffer less when compared to those who bury their worry deep inside them and get traumatised each and every second in their life.

Judith Lewis Herman opines that, "The conflict between the will to deny horrible events and the will to proclaim them aloud is the central dialect of psychological trauma" (*Trauma and Recovery* Introduction). So it is evident that expressing painful thoughts and feelings may help reduce the risk of mental illness. Rather than covering their mind with the traumatic scars, people should come out of them through revealing their scars.

The present paper "Imposed Reticence: A Delve into J. M. Coetzee's *Disgrace*" attempts to accentuate the importance of talking. Talking does not mean that the listener can solve the problem but still unveiling the darkest corners of mind to the ray of hope can heal the wounded minds to some extent. Speaking about the deepest wounds may let them go away with the wind and effaces the traces of the interrupted minds. The paper also tries to emphasise the importance of counseling and medical aids for a person who has undergone the nightmarish event that is powerful enough to shatter the ascribed meaning of their whole life.

Works Cited

Primary Source

Coetzee, John Maxwell. *Disgrace.* Vintage Publishers, 1999.

Secondary Sources

vander Kolk, Bessel A. *The Body Keeps the Score: Brain, Mind, and Body in the Healing of Trauma.* Penguin Books, 25 Sept 2014.

Hermen, Judith Lewes. *Trauma and Recovery: The Aftermath of Violence.* Basic Books. 11 June 1992.

CHAPTER 17

Tale of Trauma: The Resurfacing of the Past in Neil Gaiman's *The Ocean at the End of the Lane*

Sheethal Teresa Joseph

Literature is replete with the tradition considering traumatised child, the contemporary literature is influenced by standard constructs and focuses on the relationship between trauma and child's imagination. The portrayal of childhood trauma is laced throughout the novel, *The Ocean at the End of the Lane* as a narrative of childhood trauma. The complex meditation on trauma, survivors processing and communicating their pain is often unheard by others and are conveniently forgotten. Trauma is tenacious; it is ingrained in the circuits of our lives and the power structures of our society; it is present everywhere and does not diminish. It dwells in the soil of towns or in the water, which is the source of the greatest terror. As a 42-year-old man, the narrator gets re-traumatised by evoking memory while he drives through the lane to attend the funeral of his father. The storyline is amplified by the watery inky depiction of the narrator's memories in the nexus of reality and fantasy.

Literature has had a significant impact on people's lives. It uses a powerful vocabulary to depict man's inner life. Memories, introspection, retrospection, foreshadowing, flashback, and horrific remembrances coloured by grief, wound, and trauma have a place in literature. After a traumatic encounter, imagination has an effect on the growing self. The meaning of the term trauma has been taken from a "stress or blow that may produce disordered feelings or behavior" to a "state or condition produced by such a stress or blow" (Erikson, 184). In other words, the term trauma refers to the state of mind which results from an injury. *The Ocean at the End of the Lane* is a fantasy novel which can be read as an articulation of trauma. The plot is a devastating and damaging experience of an unnamed narrator surpassing childhood and teenage. The story is retrospective in nature, the narrator in his middle age, suddenly remembers forgotten traumatic incidents happened in his life while he passes across the Lane to attend the funeral of his father. The retrospection intuits the narrator to think a lot about his own thoughts and feelings.

There is a lot of material about the metaphor reveals called childhood in literature that could be explored for tracings of childhood landscapes. In literature and film, there is some criticism on the processes of adult remembering and writing about childhood related studies, because remembering something necessitates looking back and thinking when people talk about their past memories, they frequently return to their youth, and Gaiman's *The Ocean at the End of the Lane* starts with a reminiscence

> Soon I was driving slowly, bumpily, down a narrow lane with brambles and briar roses on each side, wherever the edge was not a stand of hazels or a wild hedgerow. It felt like I had driven back in time. That lane was how I remembered it, when nothing else was... The stench of cow muck struck me as I got out of the car and I walked gingerly across the small yard to the front door... I had been here, hadn't I, a long time ago? I was sure I had. Childhood memories are sometimes covered and obscured beneath the things that come later, like childhood toys forgotten at the bottom of a crammed adult closet, but they are never lost for good (6).

The past is accessed by a memory trigger, which is manifested by the existence of the run-down farm across the lane. The narrator returns to his hometown to attend a funeral in the novel. After the funeral, he drives about town aimlessly until he finds he's back in his old neighbourhood. He drives to the end of the tiny country lane after slowing down to inspect his old childhood home. As the narrator states: "Childhood memories are sometimes covered and obscured beneath the things that come later, like childhood toys forgotten at the bottom of a crammed adult closet, but they are never lost for good" (8). As the narrator walks into the house, meets Mrs. Hempstock, and recalls Lettie, he understands that everything is slowly coming back to him, that "memories were waiting at the edges of things, beckoning" (11). As a result, he inquires about the duck pond and is directed there. When he arrives at the duck pond and notices how small it is, he recalls that Lettie used to refer to it as her ocean, which sets off a flood of recollections that the protagonist cannot and will not stop: "I remembered that, and, remembering that, I remembered everything" (13).

The narrator of the story is a seven-year-old boy whose identity and subjectivity are shaped, moulded, and defined by his relationship with his family, his nanny, the Hempstocks, and the culture and society in which he lives. Due to its coverage of difficult issues like suicide, abuse, adultery, and vices, *The Ocean at the End of the Lane* features various sequences not intended for young audiences, which are toned down and less explicit, largely because they are viewed through the eyes of a child. They are not overly explicit since the child experiencing them does not fully comprehend them, which makes some of them even more captivating. The novel is classified as a Fantasy novel because it has magical and supernatural themes that are woven into ordinary life of an unspecified Sussex small town. The child narrator in *The Ocean at the End of the Lane* benefits a comfy lovable life until his family runs into financial difficulties. Despite the fact that the child has no friends, he is pleased with his family's relationships and does not seek out others. However, when his parents become more concerned about money, it results in their implicit absence from home and the hiring of a string of nannies to look after him and his elder sister. As a result, when things get bad, he finds himself in a world where he has no one to turn to for assistance. Because they aren't present to form a trusting relationship, the child has grown accustomed to relying on himself. "I do not know why I did not ask an adult about it, I do not remember asking adults about anything except as a last resort" (47). It's also shown in the following example: "I knew enough about adults to know that if I told them what had happened, they wouldn't believe me. Adults, on the other hand, rarely appeared to trust me when I revealed the truth. Why should they believe me when I say something so improbable?" (28). The narrator does not trust the adults to be around him when he needs them, but he also fears them since they have a tendency to distort reality. However, before the relationship between trauma and the imagination can be explored, it is necessary to conduct a detailed analysis of the trauma itself. The unnamed narrator as a child is unable to verbalise his trauma. The metaphor reveals the deficiency in narrator's communication regarding his painful experiences. He believes no one to form a dependable relationship as the child is used to rely on himself. He sees his father like scary adults who usually seem to notice children only when they misbehave: "I was terrified of him when he was angry his face angular and usually affable, would grow red, and he would shout, shout so loudly and furiously that it would, literally, paralyse me. I would not be able to think. He never hit me" (67). Although his father does not hit him, the effect of his shouting on the narrator is traumatic. "As in the school stories I read, misbehaviour often resulted in a caning, or the slipper, and then was forgiven and done, and I would sometimes envy those fictional children the cleanness of their lives (67). These instances depict his loss of trust in educational institutions, strict teachers and his classmates.

The imbalance of power between adults and children scares the narrator, as in the following instance, when the child narrator thinks about Ursula Monkton as "She was also an adult, and when adults fight children, adults always win" (87). "Ursula Monkton smiled, and the lightings wreathed and writhed about her. She was the storm, she was the lighting, she was the adult world with all its power and all its secrets and all its foolish casual cruelty. She winked at me" (149). The Nanny is viewed by the boy as a worldly beast who poses a threat to his life and those of his family. The child recalls the Nanny's insults and threats against him, including one threat to lock him up in the attic. The Hempstock women save him from extinction and restore order when his family denies him care and understanding, when his father becomes bigoted, his mother is away, his sister mocks and insults him, and the nanny threatens his existence. They feed, provide clothing, encourage, protect, and care for him emotionally, thereby replacing the child's absent mother and providing him with a secure environment. The mix of the actual workings of memory and the impact of trauma on the human psyche with mythological and wonderful characters and places can be understood as a plot of fantasy. The narrator ponders over the truth that, everyone who witnesses a tragic event will not be permanently traumatised. The plot centres on a narrator who describes the inside and external worlds. The significant role has been assigned since it represents the narrator's inner attitude as he recounts the story. The essential idea is that various people will react to similar situations in different ways. "Different people remember things differently, and you'll not get any two people to remember anything the same, whether they were there or not. You stand two of you lot next to each other, and they could be continents away for all it means anything" (183). These realisations of the narrator reflects the links existing between memory and formation of reality. Individual memories and their formation depend on our singularity. However, remembering the past can be also unwanted, and certain events and recollections may be buried deep in our consciousness and forgotten, especially when these are traumatic. In the novel, the instances is based on such traumatic events. It is introduced by, "I remembered that, and, remembering that, I remembered everything" (7), which serves as the beginning of the memory. It is organised around crisis and rebirth of the narrator and it is written in the first person, as a recounting or confession, enumerating the trials that have led to the hero's transformation. The hero makes a critical discovery, gains self-knowledge and self-confidence to improve his life. One of the themes of the novel is the search for personal reality through forgotten places, people, memories, as in, "I stared at the house, remembering less than I had expected about my teenage years: no good times, no bad times. I'd lived in that place, for a while, as a teenager. It didn't seem to be any part of who I was now" (4). Another important theme is the relationship and disconnectedness between adulthood and childhood, as in "I thought about adults. I wondered if that was true: if they were all really children wrapped in adult bodies, like children's books hidden in the middle of dull, long books. The kind with no pictures or conversations" (113).

The novel sets the stage for a series of trauma narratives that begin with seemingly inconsequential events and gradually ascends to the protagonist's forgetfulness. Retrospection has been given a significant role, as it conveys the narrator's inner attitude as he unveils the inner world. The narrator communicates all that is on his mind, including his feelings and thoughts. Every person's individuality is reflected in his mental imagery, misconceptions about power, ability, and identity of people. The power, ability, identity, misery, strangeness, exoticness and trauma pave the road of knowledge as he moves on in his life. The little boy goes through the life-altering, life-shattering experience of violence, injury, and harm. An event must decide the experience of an event that is outside the spectrum of human experience in order to be termed as traumatic. Typically, traumatic events are marked by a sense of powerlessness, as well as physical or emotional paralysis. All of these events had a negative impact on the young narrator. The model of narrator's development pointed towards a narrative of loss, where each day he survived, he became a little less childlike and a little more adult, children and childhood are revealed as shifting concepts throughout the novel.

The narrator's concerns in *The Ocean at the End of the Lane* begin with his family's financial difficulties. He lives in a safe, loving home at first, but as his family's circumstances deteriorate, the child loses his room and is forced to share it with his sister, as his parents rent it out to various renters. The boy is the one who tracks the opal miner who commits suicide in his father's car, because he needs to get his comic from the back seat. He is so taken aback by the deceased man's face that it keeps reappearing in his nightmares. Nobody shows up on his birthday, which does not seem to bother the narrator at first, or for his sister's mocking about it. In his fantasy world, he finds solace in literature and his pet, as he imagines himself as a fairy tale hero with his cat. His mother's employment is determined by her inability to stay at home due to financial constraints. This means a slew of nannies and a separation from his parents, both of which exacerbate the boy's loneliness. The nanny Ursula Monkton, the fierce symbol of villainy exploits the boy physically and mentally. Under Ursula's influence, the boy's father loses his temper, punishes his son, and almost drowns him in the bathtub:

> I was horrified, but it was initially the horror of something happening against the established order of things. I was fully dressed. That was wrong. I had my sandals on. That was wrong. The bath water was cold, so cold and so wrong. That was what I thought, initially, as he pushed me into the water, and then he pushed further, pushing my head and shoulders beneath the chilly water, and the horror changed its nature. I thought, I'm going to die (72).

The scene is perceived through the eyes of the seven-year old protagonist, who cannot understand how his father can act so unfatherly. The boy's horror is accentuated by the violation of the well-established order of family relationships. And when the boy finally escapes the house, he witnesses his father's adultery with the nanny, which adds to his feelings of despair, uncertainty and loss: "my parents were a unit, inviolate. The future had suddenly become unknowable: anything could happen; the train of my life had jumped the rails and headed off across the fields and was coming down the lane with me, then" (80). The Hempstocks take care of him, and when finally, Mrs Hempstock takes him home, she convinces him that his friend Lettie has gone to Australia to be with her dad, and that he attended her going away party. It helps him forget and repress all the instances of trauma, thus allowing him to cope with the guilt, fear, pain, loss and despair. "On the ability of the human brain to forget certain traumatic events depends the victim's survival, as memory loss is the brain's way to cope with trauma. The effects of trauma on memory depend on victim's age, personality, emotional history, rearing environment, predisposing factors, and the nature of the trauma may differentially contribute to the stress response including any disturbances of memory" (Joseph 172-73).

According to Freud's essay,

> The distinguishing mental features of a melancholia are a profoundly painful dejection, cessation of interest in the outside world, loss of capacity to love, inhibition of all activity, and lowering of the self-regarding feelings to a degree that finds utterance in self-reproaches and self-reviling's and culminates in a delusional expectation of punishment… the disturbance of self-regard is absent in mourning (Freud 244)

When it comes to the impact of trauma on identity, an emotional shock can cause such profound forgetfulness that personal identity is forgotten. After repeated traumatisation as a child, certain chronic forgetfulness might develop. These traumatic events however, are not lost for good, as certain stimuli can evoke the repressed memory. The narrator's return to the Hempstock's farm represents such a circumstance... The brain prioritises survival and self-protection in life-threatening or other traumatic events. The sufferers encounter a mixture that aids in the absorption and assimilation of traumatic events. Because, unlike the myth hero, after the narrator had discovered his true identity at the end of the story, he has gained an inner sense of security about himself, his body, and his life, as well as his social standing.

The Ocean at the End of the Lane depicts trauma, created by continuous stress, feelings of panic, impotence, loneliness, and betrayal, through retrospection. The location, which is reminiscent to the initial traumatic circumstance, induces a traumatic remembrance of past traumatic incidents. The novel might be viewed as an example of writing as therapy, demonstrating how art can be used as a relief valve for an overflowing psyche by translating painful occurrences into narrative language. It is the only Gaiman's novel written from the point of view of first person narrative. The narrator's name is unspecified, although it is mentioned in the novel that he had a silly pet name 'Handsome George' (135), which does not mean that his real name is George. Narrative recounting allows the child narrator in *The Ocean at the End of the Lane* to reintegrate his terrible memories and reassess his personality. The identity of the narrator is revealed as he goes through each day of his existence. The readers learn about the passage from childhood to adulthood through retrospective storytelling. The narrator has a traumatic memory, it interferes with existing memory generating a recollection of forgotten events. The cat, in keeping with Gaiman's own affinity for the animal, plays an important role in the story's conclusion. Throughout the story, the narrator is preoccupied with the cats. His thoughts and sentiments regarding the cats illustrate the complexities of his personality. The child narrator's home is described as a landscape of dullness, in contrast to the motherly Hempstocks' prospering enchanted paradise. The narrator's harsh punishments by the wicked nanny Ursula Monkton are healed via his relationship with the natural world and his connection with the Hempstocks through the power of imagination. The bed serves as a symbol throughout the narrative. The child narrator's closest environment was his bed, where he immersed himself in the world of books. It was the only place where he could be alone. When his room is made available to boarders, the bed becomes a metaphor of his survival with his wounded ego, as well as the boundary between self and the outside world. The protagonist's identity as a child and an adult is shaped by a variety of tangible and invisible objects. As a result, *The Ocean at the End of the Lane* is a darkly enchanting tale about memory and childhood.

Works Cited

Erikson, Kai. *Notes on Trauma and Community*. 183-99. Web.

Freud, Sigmund. *Mourning and Melancholia*. London: Hogarth Publication, 1953. 243-258.Web

Gaiman, Neil. *The Ocean at The End of the Lane*.UK Hachette Publications, 2013.

Joseph, R. "Traumatic Amnesia, Repression and Hippocampus Injury due to Emotional Stress". 169-172.n.d. Web.

CHAPTER 18

Locating the Relocated: A Psychoanalytic Perspective on Jamaica Kincaid's *Lucy*

M. Vijila Thanga Malar and Dr. R. Janatha Kumari

Caribbean literature enunciates the peculiar history of the Caribbean and the historical realities of the era. Caribbean literature includes all Caribbean territories' literary works written in English, Spanish, French, Dutch and Creoles. The writers of Caribbean Island settle in the United Kingdom, the United States and Canada for publishing their work to make a livelihood. Though the natives settle in various European countries, they write about their native culture and people in their works. Jamaica Kincaid is one of the prominent writers in the Caribbean and is considered an Antiguan writer. Caribbean writers picture the agony, pressure and pain of the individual self and long to live in the society.

Kincaid illustrates in her novel, the dynamics of female complicity with colonial patriarchy in Antigua and the English-speaking Caribbean among which are the dynamics of gender and alienation among women. Kincaid picturizes the daily dynamics of gender oppression, which is persuaded by both men and women. There is a dramatisation of the physical and psychological scar of gender and sexual inequality left by patriarchal rule in Antigua. Self-concept and self-esteem of the individual arouse from a point to develop personally to prove themselves. Their situation is to overcome the anger, personality and feelings from the immature state to become powerful from the powerless. Ironically and inadvertently, an oppressive and convoluted gender system is the source of anger that can be seen in the characters of Jamaica Kincaid. Lucy and Mariah try to come out powerfully with their self-esteem in *Lucy*.

The common fact about the human psyche is absolutely a meticulous work of God. It is filled with vast memories and it does not accept failure to blame his own. It remains indexing humans, who are very close to the cause of its fall. Internal feelings, motives and decisions are powerfully influenced by past experiences and stored in the unconscious of a human. Kincaid brings memories in the present life for comparing both incidents. The conscious and the unconscious mind struggle a lot to find the difference between the two selves and choose the perfect future.

Sigmund Freud, the most sensual psychoanalytic critic has pointed a method of mind investigation on the unconscious mind. He has framed a structure of theories concerning the relation of conscious and unconscious to focus the idea of the mind as two poles in the human mind. He is the one responsible for making it popular and this was one of his main contributions to psychology. Freud in the years 1900-1905, developed a topographical model of the mind, that describes the features of the mind namely conscious, preconscious and subconscious. Freud, in *The Unconscious* published in 1915 described "conscious mind in the unconscious which consists of all the mental processes of which one are aware, and this is seen as the tip of the iceberg. For instance, one may feel thirsty at a moment and decides to get a drink. The preconscious contains thoughts and feelings that a person is not currently aware of, but which can easily be brought to consciousness" (194). It exists just below the level of consciousness, before the unconscious mind. The preconscious is like a mental waiting room, in which thoughts remain until they "succeed in attracting the eye of the conscious" (306)

According to Freud, the unconscious mind is the primary source of human behaviour. Mild emotional experiences are in the preconscious but in some cases, traumatic and powerful negative emotions are repressed and hence, not available in the preconscious. The unconscious mind comprises mental processes that are inaccessible to consciousness that influences judgements, feelings or behaviour.

Freud discovered that his 'Topographical Model' or the concept of conscious, preconscious and unconscious mind was too simple to describe the human personality so he went on to develop the 'Structural Model,' which divided personality into three psychic apparatus to govern human behaviour: The Id, the Ego and the Superego. The Id is regarded as entirely unconscious; while the Ego and the Superego as conscious and preconscious are fully aware of what is going on in the conscious mind, we have no idea of what information is stored in the unconscious mind. The unconscious mind contains all sorts of significant and disturbing which we need to keep out of awareness because they are too threatening to acknowledge.

The conscious mind lies just above the surface of the water like the tip of an iceberg and occupies only one-tenth of human total mental life. The ideas, thoughts and images that one is aware of at any moment of the mental life are said to lie within this upper layer of his mind. Just beneath the conscious layer lies the preconscious or the subconscious mind. This middle portion of the mind stores all types of information just beneath the surface of awareness and is inactive or untapped which can be easily brought to the level of consciousness at a moment's notice whenever required. In the middle bed or layer of the human mind there lies all experiences or knowledge which have been gained or learned by an individual through various types of experiences or training. Below the preconscious mind lies the unconscious, the most important part of our mind. It is related to the vast part of our mental life which is hidden and usually inaccessible to the conscious. It contains all the repressed wishes, desires, feelings, drives and motives, many of which relate to sex and aggression. All these repressed and forbidden desires and ideas are not destined to lie permanently in the unconscious. They usually strive and agitate to come up to the preconscious or the conscious layers of the mind, sometimes in disguised forms, in dreams and reveries. This hidden treasure of mental life belonging to the unconscious is thus responsible for most of our behaviour and in fact, as Freud asserts that what we do and how we behave is always determined by the forces residing in our unconscious and not by the choices of the conscious.

According to Freud, the Id is unconscious by definition. It is the dark, inaccessible part of our personality, what little one knows of it have been learned from the study of the dreamwork and of the construction of neurotic symptoms, and most of that is negative and can be described only as a contrast to the Ego. One approaches the Id with analogies and calls it chaos, a cauldron full of seething excitations. It is filled with energy reaching it from the instincts, but it has no organisation, produces no collective will, but only a striving to bring about the satisfaction of the instinctual needs subject to the observance of the pleasure principle. He believed that sexual and aggressive drives were the most important instinctual determinants of personality throughout life.

The Ego is the organised part of the personality structure that includes defensive, perpetual, intellectual-cognitive, and executive functions. Originally, Freud used the word Ego to mean a sense of self but later revised it to mean a set of psychic functions such as judgement, tolerance, reality testing, control, planning, defence, synthesis of information, intellectual functioning, and memory. The Ego is in constant contact with time, space and physical reality. The Ego mediates among the demands of the Id, the realities of the world, and the demands of the Superego.

The third part of the personality is the Super-ego which judges whether actions are right or wrong. It is the agency that internalises the parental influences and ideals of society through early childhood experiences. It is the individual's conscience, as well as the image of the morally ideal person which is also called the ego ideal. It represents the ideal rather than the real and strives for perfection. It works following the moral standards authorised by the agents of society. The Super-ego works in contradiction to the Id. The Super-ego strives to act in a socially appropriate manner, whereas the Id just wants instant self-gratification. The Super-ego controls our sense of right and wrong and guilt. It helps us fit into the society getting us to act in socially acceptable ways.

The three components of personality are often in conflict: The Ego postpones the gratification that the Id wants immediately, and the Super-ego battles with both the Id and the Ego because behaviour often falls short of the moral code it represents. In the well-integrated personality, the Ego remains in a firm but flexible control; the reality principle governs. In terms of his earlier Iceberg model, Freud proposed that all of the Id and most of the Ego and Super-ego are submerged in the unconscious and that small parts of the Ego and Super-ego are either in the conscious or in the preconscious.

Kincaid's *Lucy* serves as a psychoanalytic novel of a young generation who gets a turn from the teenage to adulthood without parental care. Lucy's decision about life at her arrival to North America and the turn she takes after a year to wipe off the traumatic situations is deliberately illustrated throughout the novel. Self-concept themes in her novels are expressed from a different perspective.

Features such as personality, skills and abilities, physical characteristics, occupation and hobbies are assessed and applied in the novels of Jamaica Kincaid, which are ideas of oneself in a dimension.

In *Lucy,* Lucy's major source of anger is female-based and points to her mother, whom she detests. Lucy is a young newly arrived African-Caribbean immigrant from Antigua, serves as a nanny for a wealthy white couple in North America. Lucy hates her mother because whatever things she perceives as unreasonable restrictions were imposed on her by her mother. The rules, imposed under British tradition and rule during Lucy's formative years in Antigua, proves to be counterproductive to Lucy's growth and development as a young woman.

The restriction imposed the hatred of it and the sudden freedom for doing everything according to the mind at the age of 19 and the after-effects can be seen in *Lucy*. Lucy neglects to write a letter to her mother and to an extent she did not read the letter from her mother. She often mates with so many boys and finds sexual pleasure, the knowledge of which kept her mother far apart from the daughter.

Lucy's abundant freedom in immigrant land and the reaction of her unconscious mind after leaving Mariah's house shows that she is reeling in trauma. She has to take a turn to protect herself out of it. Lucy's violent motives, immoral urges, selfish needs, irrational wishes and shameful ideas, all take joint actions in the new land with Peggy. Even in Mariah's house, reading the first letter of her mother, she says, "I did not care about that any longer" (31). She did not care about sentiments. She gives priority to sexual desire and had contact with Tanner, Paul and some other boys she meets with Peggy. In a situation, her self-conscious voices to come out of the life she has chosen for mental freedom for the sake of the future. Lucy speaks as, "I had been a girl of whom certain things were expected, none of them too bad: a career as a nurse, for example; as a sense of duty to my parents; obedience to the law and worship of convention. But in one year of being away from home, that girl had gone out of existence" (133). In a hurry, she corrects her way to live an ideal life.

Lucy's self-awareness, speaks more about her character in society. She searches for the immediate changes, she made in her life in the year after immigration. She realises that her external behaviour alone has undergone the changes and the real mind was not battered. She recreated the mind to act as strong, wise and knowledgeable. Lucy avers, "The person I had become I did not know very well. Oh, on the outside everything was familiar" (133). The search for her identity gives a result out of her unconscious and the preconscious intuition is the real identity. Lucy says, "I understood that I was inventing myself and that I was doing this more in the way of a painter than in the way of a scientist… I did not have anything in the mind… I did not have a position; I did not have money at my disposal. I had memory, I had anger, I had despair" (134). As a mature girl, a year later, she lives a life according to her Caribbean society.

Lucy has severed most of her emotional agonies in North America. Though she seemed to be enjoying her new life, some of the characters that Lucy has taken up and encountered are more out of her rebellion. The difficult and repressive relationship she had with her mother under British colonial rule in Antigua plays a larger role to leave her native land. Lucy's anger due to self-esteem is peaked when she did not respond to any of her mother's letters. She learns from a family member that her father died in Antigua and left her mother without any income. Angrily and reluctantly, Lucy sends her mother some of the money she has saved for an apartment. According to Lucy, men are selfish. She never had any love for the men she saw around her either in Antigua or in the United States. The couple Mariah and Lewis, with whom she lives, move towards the end of their marriage. So, she concludes that men will not care about his family.

Lucy moves not only from her mother but also from the British patriarchal society. She hates the ideas which are thrust in the Caribbean natives. Freud states in his *The Interpretation of Dreams*, "Your previous training has given your mental activity a definite bent which leads you far away from psychoanalysis" (13). Lucy's hates Daffodils and her anger about this is best seen in her reaction in reading Wordsworth's poem *Daffodils*. As a ten-year-old girl on a tropical island, Lucy was forced to memorise and recite *Daffodils* approved by Queen Victoria Girls' School. The flower, which do not grow in the Caribbean, is symbolic of the many ways to British culture which had been forced upon the school kids of Antigua to study. After reciting the poem, Lucy tried to repress all its lines. She is surprised when Mariah's mentioning of daffodils unleashes strong emotions. She says, "I had forgotten all of this until Mariah mentioned daffodils, and now I told it to her with such an amount of anger I surprised both of us" (9). Later, when Mariah again stresses the issue of these flowers, Lucy finds that she wants to kill them. With a wave of anger, she says, 'There was such joy in her voice as she said this, such a music, how could I explain to her the feeling I had about daffodils – that it wasn't exactly daffodils, but that they would do as well as anything else?' (10).

Finally, Lucy can push this anger into full consciousness as she explains to Mariah, "Mariah, do you realise that at ten years of age I had to learn by heart a long poem about some flowers I would not see in real life until I was nineteen?' (11). The voice of Lucy is very silent in the foreign land where she has to work for her survival. Her self-concept and self-esteem warn her to follow patiently throughout. But in a circumstance, it starts speaking with a self-reflective nature which arouses her psyche to prove her to be self-potential. Lucy's self-concept can also be judged from two angles. The disability to obey the traditional rules for women is insisted on by her mother and setting herself free in the society whereto she migrated and blamed her mother for the same. She did not wish to live a life in the shadow of Mariah. Her behaviour, similar to her mother and also as a kind friend made Lucy decide to come out of Mariah's house. Lucy's self-concept lies in showing her individuality in the powerful society.

Lucy finds that she was not under the terms of the social life standard for a year and negatively moved to the irrational wishes. After a year, she gets self-awareness regarding her life and her behaviour. She changes her attitude towards life that is, to be a faultless Caribbean woman. The sense of duty arouses in her mind and conventionally she follows both cultural and religious aspects. There is no pain in the internal soul of Lucy when she reaches from where she has paused from her traditional behaviour. The real pain appears only by remembering the one year of selfish needs and irrational wishes.

Lucy is well in hand with many activities. Her social behaviour is very well designed by her mother. Even small words from her lips are monitored and justified. She avoids speaking negatively to anyone. She decides a virtuous path and plans to move forward in the future. Lucy earns money and goes out to live a life without any restriction. Lucy decides to work in a company as a receptionist to prove her individuality.

Freud opines, "Opposition between ideas is only an expression of struggles between the various instincts" (110). Lucy's search for free life is not a harmful thing unless she looks for irrational ideas. Later, she regrets and finds a righteous trial in a short period by finding a job as a receptionist. This loyal footpath marks her self-esteem to pave the future. Scrutinising the past in the present and working for a better future is highlighted in Kincaid's *Lucy*. Search for identity is an ongoing process in the novel and her character Lucy emerges as a perfect individual as a Caribbean woman. Kincaid visualises the effect of trauma in the lives of her people in the novel. The protagonists endure all the pain and pressure only to emerge as successful individuals to follow the will of their minds.

Work cited

Freud, Sigmund. *New Introductory Lectures on Psychoanalysis.* Trans. James Starchy: Penguin Books, 1991.

.... *The Unconscious.* SE, 1915.

.... *A General Introduction to Psychoanalysis,*1916-1917.

.... *On Psychopathology*, K.R.J. Book International, 2003.

Kincaid, Jamaica. *Lucy*. Farrar, Straus, and Giroux, 1990.

CHAPTER 19

Shuggie Bain: A Tale of Trauma Portrayed by Douglas Stuart

M.M. Shameema and Dr. Rohini. K. Potti

Shuggie Bain by Douglas Stuart created great discussions in the field of literature when it was first published in 2020. The world was in the fear of the spreading pandemic and people were reporting many psychological impacts. At that time, the story of a boy and his alcoholic mother attracted several readers. It became a sensational topic when it was awarded with the Booker Prize. But what made Douglas Stuart to write the novel, was the real question. He used *Shuggie Bain* as a relief book, where he poured out the suppressed feelings of his traumatic past. That is why *Shuggie Bain* had a chance to be read as a work worthy enough to be a tale of trauma.

Trauma theory aims to understand how traumatic events are depicted, absorbed, revealed, and suppressed across a wide spectrum of textual sources. If we analyse this novel on the basis of trauma literature, we will be able to find that, all the characters are somehow struggling because of the traumatic experiences they faced in life.

In the case of the author, it is a well-known fact that, Douglas Stuart wrote *Shuggie Bain* not as a way to be a good author, but to express the suppressed feelings of his heart through writing. His life was so tough that, he was already fighting with the world from his childhood itself because of his sexual identity. He was gay, and in a society where even now homosexuality is a taboo, it was really difficult for him to survive in those days of his childhood. Those abuses and bullying from others were really torturing him, whereas at home all he had was an alcoholic mother whom he loves so much.

Firstly, it is difficult to live in a home where a parent is alcoholic, here for him, she was the person he loved the most in his whole world, and so to see her struggle was the most painful experience of his life. He did everything he could to keep her happy, but her sudden death was a destructive blow to his life. After that unfortunate incident, he tried to thrive alone as much as he could. But the suppressed pain of the trauma he faced was too heavy for him to carry. Unexpressed emotions never die, instead they are buried alive and come forth later in uglier ways.

That is what Freud also said about Trauma, that while evaluating psychoanalytically, trauma is something that is so overwhelming at that moment that it cannot be easily processed by a normal person at the time of its occurrence, so that its memory is effectively blocked but returns to haunt the victim until it is properly confronted and dealt with. Douglas Stuart also went through this stage, and so for confronting his trauma, the method he chose was that of writing. He poured his pain into this novel. So that when one read *Shuggie Bain*, Shuggie and his life resembles Douglas Stuart's life in many ways.

Just like Stuart, Shuggie is also homosexual and was severely bullied by other kids. Agnes, Shuggie's mother also resembles Stuart's alcoholic mother. Same as Shuggie, Stuart also lived all alone from a very young age itself. The main point is the place where Shuggie lives, the place and the era where both Shuggie and Stuart lived are same-Scotland of Thatcher era. One can consider Scotland as one of the main characters in *Shuggie Bain*. So with all those similarities itself, one can easily assume that Stuart actually poured his life into this masterpiece. To face the trauma, he used this novel very well as a testimony.

The place which Douglas Stuart cherishes the most is Scotland. His love for that place was clearly seen throughout the work. But the time of 1980s was not an easy period for the people who lived there. Steelworks, coal mines, engine factories, and other heavy businesses closed in the 1970s and early 1980s, under the Thatcher rule, bringing the city's history to a halt. As a result, there was widespread unemployment and widespread urban deterioration. Because of the unemployment, people started to find other ways to satisfy their needs. The city was modern, but was decaying because of the lack of works and rising crimes. People fought for the allowance money granted by the government. Even women found reasons to earn money to survive.

They did every sort of things to survive without thinking whether it is good or bad. They took out their stress in such a way that we can see in the story, most of the people in the area where

Agnes and Shuggie lived in Pithead, were having a hard time as the coal mines were closed. The trauma they went through made them so miserable and pitiful.

The main character of the novel, Shuggie Bain, whose name itself is the title of the work is one of the best examples for someone who lived a whole childhood of misery because of the trauma he experienced, and survived till the end only because of his will power. He was the result of Agnes and Shug's toxic relationship. He went through a lot because of his family. He was born into that family where his mother was a depressed alcoholic and his father was an abusive man who tortured and left his mother when Shuggie was a little kid. So he had to take care of her. He always had only one thought that, if he tries harder, there will be a chance for his mother to change and live a normal life like others. Thus he took every opportunity to stay beside her and care for her.

To live with an alcoholic parent is one of the toughest things a child can bear. The chances of a kid to face trauma is very high if either of his parent is addicted to substance abuse. In the case of Shuggie, that alcoholic parent was the most precious person of his life. He loved no one else more than his mother Agnes: "…Too many days sat at her feet, just waiting and watching…Some mornings she would wake up with a fright and find Shuggie staring at her" (127). He never hesitated a moment to care for her, even after missing out his school hours.

Shuggie's brother was also depressed because of his family situations but never expressed it to anyone and just kept living a lonely life without letting anyone near him. Alexander was taken away from his biological father and he had to sacrifice his dreams because of his family situations. It made him an introvert who kept everything hidden inside himself. It is also the trait of trauma, which make individuals to grow silent and introvert after experiencing traumatic incidents. His sister left her family behind seeking for her own happiness and never returned even after hearing her mother's death. In the case of Catherine, she tried to resort to the escapism method to break the chains of traumatic memories. Due to her family situations, Catherine was also traumatised, but she chose to run far away from her family, so that she can escape from the trauma-triggering-memories in her family.

Without anyone to share his true feelings, Shuggie was surrounded by people who only exploited him. He never had any real friends except Leanne. All the kids just abused and tortured him by beating, cursing, calling him wee-poof and spitting on him because of his not-so-masculine attitude: "But he knew the McAvennie girls, and he knew their brothers would be hiding amongst the council bushes. They kept coming to the door, and when he stopped answering they took to spitting through the letter box…" (361).

In fact he himself was not aware why he was like that. Just like everyone he too thought there was something wrong about him. He was not able to understand that he was in a stage of gender nonconforming. Children who are gender nonconforming are mostly bullied by people around them. They are more likely to be excluded and verbally abused by others, and they have greater rates of depression and post-traumatic stress disorder. Boys who are recognised as homosexual and effeminate report greater childhood sexual abuse. But all these causes great psychological trauma to the kids. Shuggie just suffered everything silently.

The elders were also no different towards him, actually they were the worst, and they just took advantage of him physically:

> Slowly the driver's arm went lower down the boy's side. With a slow hand, he pulled the back of Shuggie's shirt from his tweed trousers and insidiously pushed his fat warm fingers down the back of Shuggie's underpants. Without looking, Shuggie could tell the man was still smiling at him. (316)

All Shuggie could do was to endure everything and remain silent. But no one understood that, if a child undergoes sexual abuse in his childhood, that trauma will last in him as a memory equal to a nightmare and will disrupt his character and destroy his trust in others. He had no one to play with and no one to share his secrets or pain. To live such a life is hard even for a grown-up person. But Shuggie was just a little kid, that too a kid with insecurities with his own body and his family. The level of stress he underwent is too much for a normal person to handle.

Shuggie's life was never easy. According to scientific study, if we try to categorise the mental status of Shuggie, we could firstly say that surely all those experiences made a great traumatic effect in his life. While evaluating trauma, we can assume that Shuggie had complex Developmental Trauma, which is when broad range of adverse events occur in childhood, such as being abandoned, rejected, deceived, abused, endorsing great loss of loved one, being forced etc.. As most of these things already happened to Shuggie, one may assume his mental status as the same.

In children like Shuggie, when a traumatic incident takes place, they lead to Child Traumatic Stress Disorder in them. Children with the disorder have been subjected to one or more traumas during their lives and have complex reactions that last and influence their everyday lives after the events have passed.

In *Shuggie Bain*, in the beginning pages, we can see that, Shuggie is working at a supermarket deli counter, and there while cutting the chicken, he controls himself from the urge to do the same with the customers: "In reality, pushing the metal through the bumpy pink flesh was the easy part; the difficult part was resisting the urge to do the same to the customers" (4). Those lines show that the frustration he holds inside him is still there, he just learned to hide it well. Because even after his mother's death, the world is still the same with him, they are still cruel and greedy. So the stress is still there, but now he just learned to cope up and live with it. The suppressed feeling of trauma is one of the main causes that a person is unable to step outside the boundaries of the trauma.

A devastating trauma Shuggie had was the loss of his mother. She was the only person he had from the beginning to the end to love him intensely. He withstood her alcoholic habits and struggled with her in all her difficulties. He never left her, until the day she kicked him out of their home. He blamed himself for not being able to try harder to make her quit drinking: "I think the drink will kill her, and I feel like it's my fault" (393).

He was very loyal to her. Already her drinking habit was ruining him deeply, as he was missing the care of a mother and the gentleness a kid needed while growing. Still, he was happy that, at least she is there with him. So, when she died suddenly, it broke him completely. Even after years, he is not able to cope up with the fact that she is no longer with him. Losing someone they love the most is always a devastating trauma a person may face in life.

Every time when something happens with Shuggie, it reminds him of her. The memories of Agnes, is something he can't leave behind. Just like that, all those years where he lived bearing all the bullying and sexual abuse made him a loner in the society. He has no group of friends or anyone he trusts enough to share his painful memories. The same is what Freud and Breuer stress in their work

Studies in Hysteria, the original incident may not be so traumatic at that instant than its memory. Its memory will hurt the person every moment he lives with that trauma. Only by talking about it, and confronting it themselves, they can actually face it bravely and cure it. But the one main thing is that, Shuggie was never able to talk about his Trauma to anyone. He was afraid to show his true self to anyone, in the fear that they too will take advantage of him.

Shuggie is still living a life with the painful traumatic memories; his memory is inflicted with the painful moments from where an escape is impossible. So by all these aspects too one can say that, more than Shuggie being a gay kid who thrives all the adversities of his life and move forward, Shuggie is just a kid who suffered many traumatic events in his life and is still struggling to surpass the trauma he faced. But now he has a goal in life, to be a professional hair dresser, and befriend Leanne. He is trying his level best to survive in this cruel world.

If there are two main traumatic characters in *Shuggie Bain*, then they are surely Shuggie and his mother Agnes. If Shuggie can be categorised as that kid who thrived through his trauma, Agnes is that one person, who at last surrendered to the devastating effects of the traumatic experiences she faced. The main cause of her trauma was her husband itself. She was in a toxic relationship with Shug. When she left her first husband, all she thought was that, she will be finally able to live a free life with Shug. That is the one thing she hates to remember. But those memories were still hurting her pride deeply: "All these years later, Agnes didn't want to think about that night because it made her feel like a fool" (88).

Things were really complicated with Shug. He abused her in all ways. Shug maintained illegitimate relations with other women: "She had caught him out like that once before. When he was supposed to be working a day-shift he had been upstairs fucking some unknown wifey" (76).

Shug's infidelity devastated the soul of Agnes. She was a completely different person after meeting him. Her identity was destroyed after the series of traumatic experiences she faced because of Shug. The lively woman whom every man craved for and looked upon is now a depressed alcoholic wife whom everyone scorns because of her spoiled attitude.

Shug used every opportunity to hurt her. He used to force her until she bleed and didn't even dared to look at her once whether she is okay or not. He made her feel like she was nothing without him. So that, even after knowing his infidelity, she craved for him, obsessing over the telephone to contact him. But still he was not interested in keeping her with him. Instead all he did was to get her a house and leave her there: "She knew he would never come back if she returned to her mother's. She was to stay where she was dropped. She was to take any little kindness he would give" (106).

All those completely distorted the character of Agnes. She became obsessive and violent. She started to drink heavily forgetting her family and others around her. She was good with everyone who drank with her. Others were just irritating according to her. The trauma she faced was eating her self-identity. She was not able to control it. Her two kids, Leek and Catherine went away from her, still she thought they too hated her, that is why they left her. She was not able to bring any change in her because she was under the control of the pain the traumas caused in her life. That is what trauma theorists say about trauma- it alters the person's identity.

Agnes hid her pain and loneliness in her own heart, by wearing shiny clothes and keeping her head high in front of everyone. But still slowly everyone left her. When she joined an anti-alcohol community, quit drinking and got a lover, who was gentle and caring, even Shuggie thought that she might change forever. But that too was temporary. Because, only quitting alcohol was not a cure for her. The alcohol was never a reason for her pain; it was just an escape method she used. The real reason was the traumas she faced. So all other things to keep her well became just temporary tools, as the pain of the trauma was still inside her. As Freud said, it is not possible to escape from the clutches of trauma until we confront it. By her attitude and mental stress, one can say that she was actually suffering from complex Post Traumatic Stress Disorder. So it was difficult for her to get away from the trauma and lead a normal life. The result also was as expected; she finally started to attempt suicide- because it was hard for her to escape from herself.

Agnes was never left with a good memory by anyone. She was even raped once when she was drunk: "Agnes then told Jinty the story of the bingo and the taxi and the driver pulling over into the Pit mouth. She lifted the sleeve on her jumper and showed Jinty the finger marks the rapist had left in her white skin" (202). The sexual trauma she underwent was beyond anyone else's imagination. It was obvious that the trauma left her with nothing and so she felt terribly lonely and helpless, which made her think of ending her own life.

Agnes's life was not an easy one. She tried to stay strong till the end, but the trauma she was suppressing inside her, made her terrible. The magnitude with which trauma can destroy a person's memory and identity is incalculable. The reason behind her violent behavior was nothing other than the Post Traumatic Stress Disorder and the traumatic memories with which she was living. She was not able to confront the trauma, and as a result she died at an early age. This shows the typical life of a person with trauma, only a few get an opportunity to confront their traumas and live a better life.

The devastating effect of trauma is unimaginable. It varies from person to person. As the individual and their life situations changes, the effect of trauma on that person also changes. Literature is more elaborate in displaying the innate emotions in a more delicate way, when it comes to trauma-triggering experiences. It is able to express those emotions, which maynot actually be understood at the moment when they experience the trauma. So for readers, it is actually a very memorable experience to witness such detailed emotions. That is why one can surely say that trauma literature is actually a therapy for the traumatised.

Here while reading *Shuggie Bain*, one can experience that feeling. The trauma of the author is confronted while writing the novel. The author re-experiences all those traumatic memories while writing, and thus relieve the stress he holds. Similarly, the reader gets to feel those subtle emotions which are very elaborate as if one is really experiencing it, and thus gets an opportunity to re-live those experiences and feel compassion towards the traumatised. It helps the world to understand that, everyone is struggling a battle of their own and it is our need to be gentle and kind towards others; because sometimes two good ears are enough to save the life of a suffering individual.

Works Cited

Stuart, Douglas. *Shuggie Bain.* Picador, 2020.

Bruer, Joseph, and Sigmund Freud. *Studies in Hysteria.* Translated by A. A. Brill, Beacon Press, 1895, pp. 3-13, *Internet Archive,* 2006, ia801606.us.archive.org/35/items/in.ernet.dli.2015.151941/2015.151941.Studies-In-Hysteria.pdf. Accessed 7 March 2021.

Freud, Sigmund. *The standard edition of the complete psychological works of Sigmund Freud.* Translated by James Strachey, E-book, vol. 1, p.169, The Hogarth Press, 1999.

Contributors

1. **Asha P. V.**, Assistant Professor of English, Central Polytechnic College, Trivandrum.
2. **Athira. S. S**, Assistant Professor, Department of English, Malankara Catholic College, Mariagiri.
3. **Dr. Manju R.** Assistant Professor, Department of English Government College, Nedumangad, Trivandrum.
4. **Dr. N.U. Lekshmi**, Assistant Professor of English, Sree Ayyappa College for Women, Chunkankadai. (Affiliated to Manonmaniam Sundaran ar University, Tirunelveli.).
5. Dr. **R. Janathakumari**, Assistant Professor of English, Sree Ayyappa College for Women, Chunkankadai. (Affiliated to Manonmaniam Sundaranar University, Tirunelveli.).
6. **Dr. Reji A. L,** Assistant Professor, Department of English, MES Keveeyam College, Valanchery, Malappuram.
7. **Dr. Rohini. K. Potti**, Assistant Professor, Department of English, Government College, Kasaragod.
8. **B. Sajeetha**, Assistant Professor, Department of English and Research Center, Sree Ayyappa College for Women, Chunkankadai. (Affiliated to Manonmaniam Sundaranar University, Tirunelveli).
9. **Dr. Sheeba S Nair**, Assistant Professor, Department of English, Sree Ayyappa College for Women, Chunkankadai. (Affiliated to M.S. University, Tirunelveli).
10. **K. S. Chitra,** II MA English, Sree Ayyappa College for Women, Chunkankadai.
11. **M. M. Shameema**, II MA English, Government College, Kasaragod.

12. **Monisha M**. Ph.D. Research Scholar, Sree Ayyappa College for Women, Chunkankadai, Kanyakumari. (Affiliated to Manonmaniam Sundaranar University, Tirunelvel).
13. **Ms. Anju.** M. B, Assistant Professor, Post Graduate Department of English, Government College Tripunithura.
14. **Nayana. N.V**, Research Scholar, Muslim Arts College, Thiruvithancode, Manonmaniyam Sundaranar, University, Abishekapatti, Tirunelveli 627012, Tamilnadu.
15. **Neethu A. Nair**, Full-Time Research Scholar, Assistant Professor and Research Guide, Register No: 20213184012004 Department of English and Research Centre, Sree Ayyappa College for Women Chunkankadai, Nagercoil (Affiliated to Manonmaniam Sundaranar University, Thirunelveli, 627012), Tamil Nadu, India.
16. **Rajasree R**., Assistant Professor, Department of English, Sanatana Dharma College, Alappuzha.
17. **Sajena A**. Research Scholar, Department of English, Sree Ayyappa College for Women, Chunkankadai. Affiliated to Manonmanium Sundaranar University, Tirunelveli.
18. **Sheethal Teresa Joseph**, MA English Language and Literature, Marthoma College, Kuttapuzha, Thiruvalla, Affiliated to MG University, Kerala.
19. **Soubhagya S.P.**, Full Time Research Scholar, Resister No: 19213184012008, Sree Ayyappa College for Women, Chunkankadai, Affiliated to Manonmaniam Sundaranar University, Abishekapatti, Tirunelveli,627012, Tamil Nadu, India.
20. **Soumya S. J,** Full Time Research Scholar, Reg No: 20213184012006, Department of English and Research Centre, Sree Ayyappa College for Woman, Chunkankadai, Nagercoil, (Affiliated to Manomaniam Sundaranar University, Abhishekapetti, Thirunelveli, 627012), Tamil Nadu, India.
21. **Sreelatha.R.H,** Research Scholar, Sree Ayyappa College for Women, Chunkankadai.
22. **V. Kezia Anna**, Asst. Prof. of English, Govt. KNM Arts and Science College.
23. **M. Vijila Thanga Malar**, Research Scholar, Sree Ayyappa College for Women.

Index